The Book of
CAKE

Celebrating Stories and Faces of Hope Network
By Tom Rademacher

This book is produced and published by

HOPE NETWORK

www.hopenetwork.org

COPYRIGHT

Published in the United States of America by Hope Network (www.hopenetwork.org)

Library of Congress Cataloging-in-Publication Data
Rademacher, Tom.
The Book of CAKE: Stories and Faces of Hope Network

p.   cm.

ISBN 978-0-9843392-1-1

Printed in the United States of America.
First Edition

Cover and Book Design by Amy Cole at JPL Design Solutions

Hope Network is a Christian organization that empowers people with disabilities and disadvantages to achieve their highest level of independence.

DEDICATION

This book is dedicated to

KATHY DUNLAP

Who for a decade has given her time, talent, treasure and heart to all served by Hope Network—unseen but present in every story told.

TABLE OF CONTENTS

TABLE OF CONTENTS *continued*

ACKNOWLEDGEMENTS

A lot of ingredients went into this Book of CAKE. Though I wrote the stories, it would have been impossible to assemble this keepsake of inspiring people were it not for the tireless efforts of more than a baker's dozen.

To Phil Weaver, president and CEO of Hope Network—thanks for taking a chance on this novel approach to highlighting the people who make Hope Network the special organization it is. I trust the product of many talented hands was worth the risk.

For staying the course, and maintaining the focus on a lively mix of Hope consumers, volunteers, benefactors, board members and more, I am indebted to Dan Holbert, Hope Network's chief administration officer.

When Mr. Weaver and Mr. Holbert were attending to the scores of other responsibilities they have with Hope, I was led down righteous paths by Hope Network Senior Administrative Assistant Sally Hall.

Thanks to those with keen eyes who helped proof and edit these stories. They are the gifted individuals within Hope Network's marketing department: Dan Gowdy, Simone Thiessen and Claudia Elzinga.

To everyone who suggested a story, my deepest appreciation. You know who you are. And if you haven't seen your story in CAKE yet, stay tuned. We're still mixing batter.

CAKE might never had existed in any form were it not for the ingenious leadership of Jim Heynen, who dreamed up the concept from blue sky. And it was Julie Spahn who laid out each story before it debuted in newsletter format. Her fingerprints are on every story.

To my instructors at Grand Valley State University, who wondered back in 1978 why I would forsake my degrees in Special Education and Psychology to pursue a lifetime of newspaper writing—here's proof of what I'd been storing in my heart all those years.

Finally, I want to offer thanks and prayers to the consumers of Hope Network who allowed me to make their private lives public. Heroes, all.

Tom Rademacher

INTRODUCTION

This book is infused with Tom Rademacher's power. A story-teller without peer, he's taken home the National Society of Newspaper Columnists' most prestigious awards when competing with the largest newspapers in the U.S. He's a gifted writer. Even more, he's an explorer who uncovers what is unique in each of us, a trustworthy friend who opens us to public view without embarrassment. For a year Tom lived with the people of Hope Network. This book is his journal.

What makes Tom's journal memorable are his subjects. In this collection, they come from Hope Network. Among many fine social services, mental health, rehabilitation and specialty agencies, Hope Network employs the word "Christian" modestly and pervasively to describe its roots, its values and its mission. It does not evangelize, nor does it need to. In labor and tears and laughter and courage, day and night, weekdays and holidays, the people of Hope Network become the Gospel to those most in need of good news.

They demonstrate, and this book makes plain, that Saint Francis was right: "Preach the gospel at all times—if necessary, use words."

Dan DeVos, Chairman
Hope Network Boards of Directors

FOREWORD

For the past five years my professional time has been spent as President and CEO of Hope Network, a Michigan-based organization with some 2,500 employees serving 25,000 individuals and families every year. In other words, I have the best job in the world.

Hope Network is at work in all sorts of communities, serving all sorts of people. But especially in Michigan, unemployment and poverty have become commonplace. Economic struggles take a toll. Fear of losing one's job, one's home and one's dignity cause pain and illness. At the same time, as public resources shrink and private dollars become more precious, we've learned to achieve savings through excellence—to be the best possible stewards of monies entrusted to us.

The people we're honored to serve—those with developmental disabilities, with traumatic and severe brain injuries, with mental illness or broken families or a prison record—truly matter. When we invest in their health, we are repaid with their employment; they join us as fellow tax-payers and independent, productive citizens. The cost of turning away from our ailing neighbors is long-term and enormous; the benefit of investing here is staggering.

Our literature tells you that Hope Network is "a Christian organization that empowers individuals with disabilities or disadvantages to reach their highest level of independence." This is our mission.

What literature struggles to explain is the power of seeing this mission come to life when the brain-injured young father rises from his wheelchair to hug his infant daughter, or the 40-year-old with Down Syndrome proudly takes home their first paycheck. The mission takes on meaning when the terrified child with Autism discovers she's in a place that is safe and loving, or the ex-offender is accepted for who he has become, not what he once did. I have the incredible joy of watching communities rally to care for those who have been despised and rejected, people of sorrow and acquainted with grief. Our mission is written most eloquently in miracles.

Tom Rademacher came to us equipped with the gifts of a writer, the heart of a father and the desire to uncover and tell stories of hope. For more than a year he sat, he listened, he wrote, and he moved us all. This collection takes us with him into the lives, the struggles, the gifts and the laughter of remarkable people—most of whom I've been honored to know.

This is the story of Hope Network told through the miracles of its people.

Phil Weaver,
President and CEO
Hope Network

AGAINST ALL ODDS

TOMMIE SPICER: NOW BATTING CLEAN-UP... AND LOVING EVERY MINUTE OF IT

In a perfect world, Tommie Spicer might have tried out for the high school football and basketball teams in his hometown of Drew, Mississippi.

Who knows; he might have gone on to diamond or gridiron stardom, even rubbed shoulders at some point with his boyhood hero, pro basketball phenom Wilt "The Stilt" Chamberlain.

But his dreams of athletic glory were dashed before he could hardly express them.

"I wanted to go out, but they wouldn't allow me to do it," remembers Tommie, whose vision was affected at an early age by retinitis pigmentosa. "I really wanted to be a baseball player, a basketball player, but my eyesight stopped me.

"I thought I was good," he says.

"But they said, 'You can't.'"

Some 40 years later, Tommie Spicer is gently stuffing "You can't" right back at anyone who ever doubted he could accomplish the things a fully sighted individual is capable of doing.

Until the mid-1980s, Tommie was able to operate a motor vehicle. But his condition, progressive in nature, has gradually rendered him almost totally blind. Today, at the age of 57, he is

incapable of distinguishing beyond light and dark, and he relies in part on a cane to make his rounds.

The story of Tommie Spicer, however, hardly concludes with a chapter on regret or unfulfillment. Instead, it is a volume packed with stories of "I can," beginning with his early days as one of eight children born to southern sharecroppers, and continuing with his ongoing employment as a custodian at Hope Network headquarters on Orchard Vista Drive SE.

Tommie was born in Sunflower County, a northwestern region of Mississippi that is largely poor, rural and home to the small town of Drew, where he grew up among fewer than 2,000 others.

His parents, Lee and Alice, relied on their brood to help feed the family, and though Tommie had vision challenges from early on, he was expected to pull his weight like everyone else.

"I guess that came mostly from my mother," he says of Alice, who is 80 and still employed as a cleaning woman. "She was a lady who believed that you can do anything you want to do if you put your mind to it.

"She didn't allow for any excuses. Even when I would say 'Mom, I can't see how to do that,' I can still hear her today telling me 'Boy, you can do it.'"

Challenges followed Tommie into the Drew public school system, where he craved to try out for high school sports teams alongside his buddies. But coaches and educators said no.

After high school, Tommie eventually wandered north into West Michigan, following in the wake of a big brother who'd just been

The story of Tommie Spicer, however, hardly concludes with a chapter on regret or unfulfillment.

discharged from the Army. He found work at a Grand Rapids factory, where he stayed 17 years. He also worked as a dishwasher at a local hotel.

His vision was worsening, though, and several years ago, he sought assistance from the Michigan Commission for the Blind (MCB). "Glasses couldn't do me no good," he recalls.

Driving was no longer possible, and shapes and figures he used to be able to discern were becoming mere blurs.

It was largely through Patricia Angerman, a rehab counselor with the MCB, and mobility specialist Jennifer Graham, that Tommie made initial gains in compensating for his debilitating vision. Patricia and Jennifer then teamed with Hope's Chelsea Irish to help Tommie qualify as the first totally blind person to successfully complete a "Green Clean" program that coaches custodians on how to perform their jobs while respecting the environment.

"One thing that I'll say about Tommie is that he'll try anything," says Patricia. "If he had any reservations, he never showed them."

Chelsea, a lead independent living instructor and evaluation technician, was equally astonished at what Tommie was able to accomplish as a member of the 15-person cleaning crew she directed at Hope's Sojourners Transitional Living Center in Ada Township.

Tommie quickly exhibited not only the skill to one day serve as a custodian, but the drive to become independent. It wasn't long before he was applying for a job so that he might shift from a Hope Network consumer to a Hope Network employee.

"My brain, I think, was very stereotypical in the beginning," says Chelsea, who initially figured Tommie would need a lot of coaching and make only small gains at first. "I didn't realize how much he'd be capable of."

What soon surfaced "was this courage and quiet dignity about him," says Chelsea, who rejoiced with many others last September when Tommie was hired as one of three who today cleans Hope's corporate facility.

Tommie with Chelsea Irish

It's not a job for the timid, given the fact that Tommie pitches in to clean everything from office space to restrooms to the kitchen to the cafeteria—and with only the slightest bit of perception between light and dark to assist him visually.

With help from Patricia and Jennifer and Chelsea, though, he's discovered ways to compensate. To distinguish among cleaning bottles that are the same size but hold different ingredients, he wraps one, two or three rubber bands around them, so he can "feel" what he's holding.

He relies on his sense of hearing, too. For example, if he's readying to clean the kitchen or cafeteria but senses an important meeting taking place at a nearby table, he'll quietly leave and alter his schedule out of politeness.

He's attached Velcro strips beside door handles to differentiate among entries leading to restrooms, offices, storage areas and more. And he employs patterns and repetitions where others are able to use sight to their advantage. He always wipes mirrors top to bottom. He sweeps and mops floor with intricate strategies designed to cover every square inch. And he memorizes the steps and number of turns that take him to virtually every nook and cranny in the building.

If he wasn't using a white cane to help himself along, you might never suspect Tommie Spicer is almost totally blind.

"I couldn't get over how Tommie was to work with," says Chelsea, "…his speed and quality of work. He works at a job that's tough for a sighted person to do, and he does it quickly and thoroughly."

"You can't not love his attitude," says Patricia Angeman. "He's just a great guy."

As for Tommie, he's got some special advice for anyone walking a tightrope between "I can't" and "I can."

"I tell 'em don't feel sorry for yourself. If you put your mind to it, you can.

"Don't give up," says Tommie. You gotta dream, and you can't ever give up on your dreams.

"You just gotta press forward."

■ ■ ■ ■ ■ ■

SIX THINGS THAT MAKE HIM TOMMIE:

1. He starts most mornings with (better take a breath!) 30 minutes on the treadmill, 150 pushups and 150 squats.

2. His favorite snack: Cake and 7-Up.

3. Tommie has 5 stepchildren with wife Joyce, who works as a nurse's aide. The couple lives on Grand Rapids' Southeast Side.

4. Guess who does the cleaning at home? Yup, Tommie. "He does a nice job with the cleaning and the dishes," says Joyce.

5. Three or four times a year, Tommie preaches before the congregation at Church of God Pentecostal on Ashland Avenue NE. He also spends precious time reading from his electronic Bible.

6. Tommie's parents didn't dote much on their kids' names. Tommie is actually Tommie James, to differentiate from older brother Tommie Lee. He's also got a brother named Willie James and a sister named Willie Jean. Most friends and family call Tommie by Tommie or Tom, but for reasons that even Joyce can't recall, she calls him Tony!

CONNIE *david*

Connie David (left) practicing a hair wash

CONNIE DAVID—
FINDING FULFILLMENT IN CHAOS

She's never late.
She never complains.
She does what's asked.

She's Connie David.

And in case you'd like to hire her, you might as well get in line; she's already on staff at Chaos Spa Salon in Cadillac.

Her role today is a million miles from where she used to be—how she used to be dismissed—as someone with challenges that somehow made her unfit for employment.

But collaboration between the salon and Hope Network of Cadillac changed all that when people looked below the surface of one special woman and realized she had gifts to give.

"She's part of the family," says salon coordinator Jana Maxwell. "Tuesdays wouldn't be the same without her."

That's the day Connie, who is in her 50s, shows up each week to work part of the morning for a salon that's emerged for her as a second home. She began there as a volunteer, but eventually demonstrated enough savvy to be placed on payroll.

It wasn't long ago that Connie bought and paid for her very first television—a moment steeped in pride and joy. "I like to shop," she says with a wide smile. "I get to spend my paycheck."

Connie, who is Native American and was born in the Traverse City area, bounced around among foster homes and other sites before moving in with Sue Armstead, who used to serve as her caregiver and now just calls her housemate.

They share a home in nearby Lake City, though no grass grows beneath either woman's feet. Sue helps out at a foster care site most days, while Connie stays busy at area workshops and other supervised settings when not contributing at Chaos.

Like most any first-time employee, Connie eased into the job, learning more each session about what was expected. "We had to remind her from time to time about things in the beginning," says salon owner Tracey Kanouse. "But now when she walks in, she goes right to it."

Which means the following: fold laundry, dust shelves, arrange product, fill guest packs, and wash the windows and mirrors.

"After that, she'll look for other things to do," says Tracey. "It's always, 'What's next?' and that's pretty cool."

In special moments, Connie will work alongside an apprentice like Jana, who is pursuing a license to work in a salon. Together, they'll shampoo, rinse, blow-dry and style a wig atop a mannequin head. "Fabulous," says Jana, as they survey a finished product, and Connie beams with joy.

Michelle Munn is a site supervisor for the Hope team in Cadillac and one of those responsible for seeing the potential in Connie.

"Connie had always wanted to work in a salon, but people pretty much told her she never would."
—Michelle Munn

"Connie had always wanted to work in a salon, but people pretty much told her she never would," Michelle relates. "We got word of that, and saw an opportunity to partner on Tuesdays at Chaos.

"Six months ago, I said to Tracey that she's really working like an employee now. So they put her on as a paid worker."

Michelle works with another half-dozen other Hope Network consumers in the Cadillac area who are picking up employment skills at everything from a bowling alley to coffee shop and deli. But Connie's story is special: "She's our first placement, and a real success story," says Michelle.

Connie isn't just part of the staff.

She belongs.

That's evidenced by the way in which she serves customers.

"The salon atmosphere is one where people come here to relax," explains Jana. We want to make sure that everything is about them. And Connie fits in so well. She'll be glad to get someone coffee, to make someone comfortable.

"She's just one of the girls."

It's getting on about noon, and time for Connie to punch out. One of the last things she does as part of her work routine is to wipe clean a pair of mirrors on the salon's south wall.

On one, there are words etched into the glass that read "BEAUTY COMES IN ALL SIZES."

Exactly.

■ ■ ■ ■ ■ ■

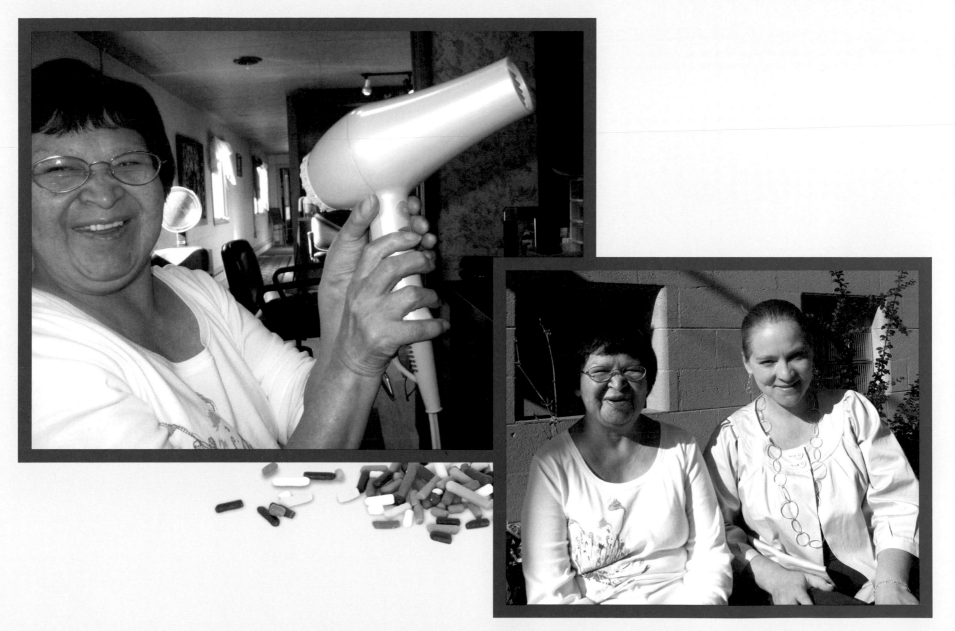

Connie with Michelle Munn

MAKING THE MOST OF A SECOND CHANCE

Jahaun McKinley points to a nondescript entrance that he and fellow employees use to access Cascade Engineering.

Then he motions to another more formal access point, smiles broadly and says, "That's the door I'll be using when I'm corporate."

In one way, it's almost implausible to consider Jahaun McKinley as a white-collar executive at an internationally respected engineering firm, given that Jahaun has spent roughly half his 38 years behind bars.

But this is one Hope Network consumer who plans to squeeze the most out of his future, making up for the 18 years and 11 months and four days he spent imprisoned for assault with intent to commit murder when he was 17 years old.

Today, Jahaun is a confident man with a goal of earning a college degree and becoming part of the administrative family at Cascade Engineering in Cascade Township, just south of Grand Rapids.

It's been a long road, though, beginning with troubling teenage years while growing up in Muskegon, then Grand Rapids. Jahaun's mother gave birth to him when she was just 16, and he was raised largely by his grandmother.

He started peddling drugs while a student at Grand Rapids Ottawa Hills High School, where he finally dropped out during the 11th grade.

possession of a firearm, which he figures "played into my conviction." He'd also spent a short time in jail for loitering in a known drug area.

Looking back, Jahaun says "I knew what I didn't do but I didn't know how to make a defense of it." His attorney, he says, urged him to plea-bargain, and Jahaun eventually admitted to a lesser charge, for which he received 20 to 60 years.

He entered prison as a bitter and angry young man of 18, and in the beginning was anything but a model prisoner. "I was a fighter," he says, which probably helped tack an extra year on the time he'd ultimately spend incarcerated.

"I just walked out of class one day," he remembers. "I was a decent student; I even tutored some kids. But I didn't have a stable home life," he says, recalling issues he had with his stepfather.

His grandmother tried to keep him on a moral track, but the wrong crowd lured him in, and things reached a boiling point one evening outside a restaurant in his former hometown of Muskegon, when more than 200 kids gathered and a fight broke out.

When the dust settled, one person was dead and several others injured by gunfire. Jahaun was initially charged with four counts of attempted murder and one count of open murder, and faced a life sentence.

A witness insisted Jahaun was the triggerman, which he refutes to this day, saying it was a case of mistaken identity. It didn't help that earlier in his teens, Jahaun had been caught with the illegal

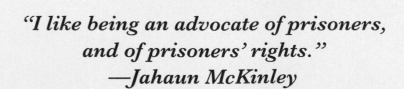

"I like being an advocate of prisoners, and of prisoners' rights."
—*Jahaun McKinley*

Two things helped transform him.

One was the prison library, where he devoured biographies of people who had ascended to power. "People who dealt with problems, the unfairness of life," he says.

Then his beloved grandmother grew sick, a woman he sometimes telephoned dozens of times monthly, the person he relied on for support and advice. "That was my final wake-up call," he says of her death in 2006. "I took it real hard, and it's then I knew I had to straighten up and get out."

He exited prison with a GED, but knew instantly that if he were to soar, he'd need advanced education. He's enrolled now at Grand Rapids Community College, with plans to earn a bachelor's degree in finance or a related field.

Upon his release in 2009, Jahaun also entered Hope Network's Workforce Development program, which in part teams with ex-offenders in an effort to secure them employment and help them re-enter the world beyond bars.

Ben Rosa, senior program manager, immediately saw potential in Jahaun. Not only did he embrace all the touchstones of the program, but eventually surfaced as a speaker to help advance the program's mission.

"He's talking to so many ex-offenders himself," Rosa says of Jahaun. "He's done several panels with me, advocating for

On the job with Mindy Ysasi

change. We're not asking for employers to treat ex-offenders any differently. Just give them an opportunity."

Jahaun applied for a job at Cascade Engineering and entered through a temporary staffing agency in April 2010. After six months, he was offered a full-time job.

Cascade Engineering, which employs about 600 here and more than 1,000 worldwide, enjoys a close relationship with Hope's re-entry program.

Mindy Ysasi, who works in Cascade's Human Resources, helped set the stage for Jahaun's employment, and says his "demeanor and work ethic fit very well into the kind of culture we're trying to develop here."

Ysasi likes to think that "We all have barriers" to certain types of employment, and that it's the responsibility of a business to reach out. Jahaun responded to that by showing up not to ask "What can you do for me?" but instead "What do I need to do?"

When Jahaun's not working a 6 p.m. to 6 a.m. shift at Cascade, he's likely studying inside his southeast side apartment for classes at GRCC, or serving on

behalf of Hope Network and others like him seeking a second chance in the workplace.

"I like being an advocate of prisoners, and of prisoners' rights," says Jahaun. "I can help destroy the image of what an incarcerated person is."

He's grateful for Hope's re-entry program, which he says equipped him with computer skills, job interview techniques, and "how to look, how to behave" in front of interviewers.

Jahaun is not one to publicly share his former life in prison, at least in large ways. But he did make an exception at the conclusion of a GRCC English composition class, where he outlined his jail time in an essay.

Asked to read his piece aloud in class, his fellow students were astonished. For his efforts, the instructor presented him with an award entitled "Best Essay for Second Chance at Life."

Ben Rosa isn't surprised. "His one life," he says of Jahaun, "is now changing others' lives."

■ ■ ■ ■ ■ ■

AL & HIS PALS—OUTGOING HOPE NETWORK CONSUMER AL CHANEY MAKES FRIENDS WHEREVER HE GOES

Peter Goetz is used to dealing with thousands of dollars at a time in his role as a salesman at Keller Ford on Alpine Avenue in northwest Grand Rapids.

But tucked away in a little slot in his work desk, he's always sure to have at least 50 cents on hand for a special friend who visits the auto dealership every week.

"He'll do a little cleaning here and there for us," says Peter. "Maybe brush some snow off some cars. I always keep a couple quarters for him, and we take care of him.

"He's a good egg, and he'd give you the shirt off his back. He's just everybody's friend."

The source of so much sunshine? Meet Al Chaney, who despite his cognitive impairment, spreads smiles and goodwill throughout the small but profound circles in which he functions outside of his Hope Network residence, located less than a mile from Keller Ford.

And the BP service station.

And the Dollar Tree store.

The Starbucks.

Family Christian Bookstore.

"High-Fives" from friends at Starbucks

You might just call Al Chaney the Ambassador of Alpine Avenue, for all the friends he's made...

Al gets "hired" for small jobs at Keller Ford

Bed, Bath & Beyond.
Payless Shoes.
And on and on and on.

You might just call Al Chaney the Ambassador of Alpine Avenue, for all the friends he's made since moving six years ago into Hope Network's "Haven," a 16-bed residential facility east off Alpine and within walking distance of dozens of stores and businesses on the busy commercial thoroughfare.

Al largely limits his walks to an area between Three and Four Mile Roads NW. But that stretch of pavement provides plenty of stops for a happy-go-lucky guy who, while enjoying the cozy room he keeps at the Haven, can't seem to get enough of the outside world.

"He'll go out for an hour, then come back, and within a few minutes, will want to go right back out again," says Marilyn Shipp, a residential instructor at the Haven. "He's just very social."

Al, 57, spent his formative years in the Saginaw area. He's one of 10 children born to a mother who loved to garden and a father who labored both in a foundry and at concrete work. "It was hard, but we did it," Al remembers of helping his dad on jobs.

He smiles broadly: "I liked the gardening more."

A lifelong bachelor, Al worked a while in a grocery store before it closed down, then made his way to the Grand Rapids area, hooking up with Hope around 2005. The Haven serves as his base of operation, where he lives with one other man and 14 women.

"When it gets to be too much," Marilyn jokingly says of all the female influence, "Al goes to his room."

Or out.

On the day I visited, Al couldn't wait to get going. "Ready, Tom? Ready, Tom?" he said as I tried to finish interviewing staff at the Haven. "Ready? Ready? Ready?"

In the next moment, we're walking, and briskly.

I ask Al if rainy or snowy days ever slow him down.

"No way, no way," says Al, and suddenly, the man who was relatively quiet in the company of so many women suddenly goes uber-verbose.

I can't make out all the words, but he ends nearly every statement with the earnest question "Right, Tom?"

And even though I'm not sure what he's said in every instance, there's a twinkle emanating from behind those eyeglasses telling me he's just enjoying the sights and sounds and effects that spring from being outdoors. "That's right, Al."

Our first stop is the BP station, where clerk Alex Bierlein breaks into a wide smile at Al's approach. "Hi Al," she says, and without much prompting, volunteers that "Al brightens it up here every day. He makes things interesting, that's for sure."

Al's just finished a soda, and he exchanges the bottle for 10 cents. Some days, Alex will treat her friend of two years with a donut or discounted cup of coffee. "You get spoiled here, don't you, Al?" she teases.

It's not unusual for Al, while visiting with Alex, to help a customer search for the right-sized cup, or an item off the shelf. "He asks everyone in line how they're doing," says Alex.

Next stop is a nearby Starbucks, and upon his entrance, Al is treated to a chorus of smiles and hellos from the green-aproned staffers.

"This man comes in and brightens our days," says Mary Nagy, who used to work here and is visiting former co-workers while sipping on a drink.

Employee Tracy Broadhurst exchanges a high-five with Al, then slips him a biscotti, no charge. Another employee raises an eyebrow, and Tracy says "Hey, it was broke," and they both smile.

"He's like our mascot," says Tracy.

"He should be U of M's mascot,"says employee Ben Garlets, and everyone agrees that most of Al's clothing—his caps and jackets— boast the familiar block M that defines the University of Michigan.

On any given day, Al might cross the street and visit friends at a shopping center anchored by the Target store. But this morning, he's settling for a visit to the Ford dealership before heading back to the Haven.

"It's a joy to have him walk through the showroom," says salesman Matt Sunderlin. "He's always so pleasant."

"We tease him about being related to Dick Cheney," says co-salesman Peter Goetz, and then he relates a story about Al that has him shaking his own head in disbelief.

"Al's been coming here ever since about 2005," says Peter. "And at one point, I was gone three full years. I came back here to work, and Al walks in, and even though it's been three years, it was 'Hey Pete, how ya doin'?'"

■ ■ ■ ■ ■ ■

Al at Haven Home with Hope Network staff
(left to right) Loretta Crisp, Ashley Wert and Marilyn Shipp

IN A NUTSHELL, AL:

1. What he does every Thursday? Buys one Lottery ticket. Has he won big? He just laughs.

2. Favorite book: The Bible

3. Chores he performs at the Haven: Shovels snow, takes out trash, hauls linen in and out

4. Games he likes to play: Checkers and cards

5. Best car on the road today: Ford

6. Church he prefers, when there's transportation: Calvary, on the East Beltline

7. Beginning to most days: Up at 6 a.m., shower, breakfast, then out the door

8. A favorite place to shop: TJ Maxx

9. Favorite song (and with a very apt title), which Al loved to perform karaoke style at a nearby restaurant before it folded: "Hit The Road, Jack!"

"KEEPING TIME" WITH MIRACLE CHILD JEFFREY RICHARDS

Some of us see miracles in the simple grandeur that is each new sunrise, a blossoming of lilacs, the arc of a rainbow.

Others celebrate the more mysterious or majestic varieties—an inexplicable cure of cancer, the transformation of someone into a brand new person.

Then there is Jeffrey Richards, who wasn't supposed to survive infancy, and against all odds, is still with us 29 years later, laughing and loving and demonstrating to us all that some miracles play themselves out from a single ripple.

Jeffrey is a man on the go, splitting his time between visits with his family in Alto, the group home he shares with five other men, and weekday activities at Hope Network's Northeast Center on Knapp Street NE.

But his story really begins with a prognosis from the medical team that predicted upon his birth in April 1982 that he had but a 15 percent chance of survival. He weighed 2 pounds, 3 ounces, required a respirator to supply his breathing, and a tube into his stomach to provide nutrients. Multiple problems attended his birth, and contributed to the tragic death of his twin brother Jared at just two days old.

Those were indescribably tough times for Jeffrey's parents, Dale and Carol, yet now they marvel at the progress their once-little boy has made.

"They told us he'd never walk," remembers Dale. "But we got him riding a bicycle, and roller blading, and everything else.

"It's a miracle, it is. His whole life has been a miracle."

Dale and Carol are unusually candid about their son's history, which first surfaced nearly three decades ago when they fought medical opinions suggesting they couldn't check Jeffrey out of the hospital at 10 months old while he was basically on life support.

The parents won, creating something of a media sensation with their insistence that they could create gains for their little boy outside a hospital.

By the time he was 14 months old, they'd weaned him from the breathing and feeding tubes, and celebrated as he crawled. By age 3, he was walking. He was slow to speak, though his parents have recordings of him babbling. His speech suffered significantly when he developed an allergic reaction to a medicine that stole away his ability to hear.

These days, he's a profound presence at the Northeast Center, where 30 Hope Network consumers congregate in five classrooms under the supervision of Center Administrator Linda Idsinga, Jeffrey's instructor Tonya West, and a dozen other staff members. The goals there are to enrich lives, build skills and create opportunities for consumers to become more a part of their community.

When Jeffrey arrived at the Northeast Center about two years ago, he was well-trained in the American Sign Language, but not so the staff. They hustled to catch up, though, and helped to create a comfortable environment for Jeffrey.

A big smile for mom and dad

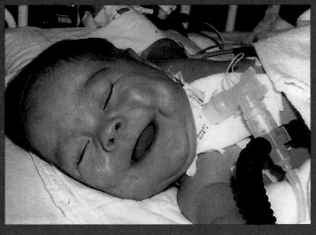

Jeffrey Richards, ...against all odds, is still with us 29 years later, laughing and loving and demonstrating to us all that some miracles play themselves out from a single ripple.

19

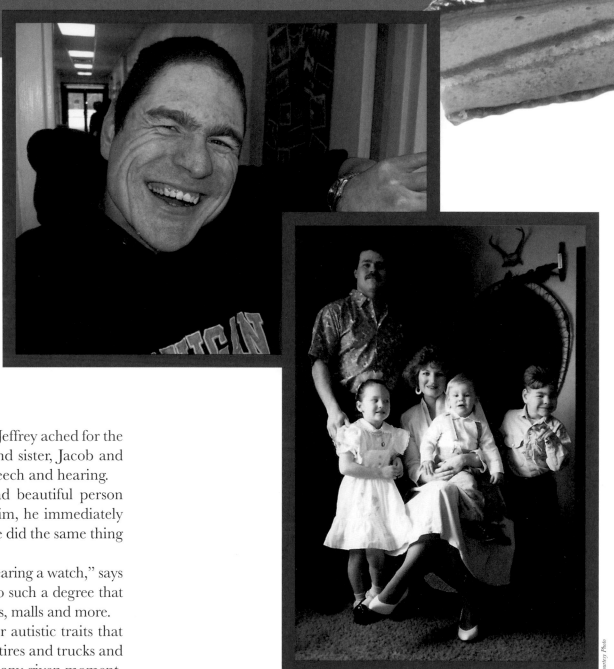

Jeffrey's parents have a special place in their hearts for the employees who help him move forward: "We don't think he'd be where he is today if it weren't for Hope," says Carol.

The Northeast Center staff also has worked hard to make it a safe environment at the Center, especially important because Jeffrey had been placed elsewhere in the past where, according to his parents, he'd been subjected to physical abuse by other students.

"We'd go to visit him," says Carol, "and he'd be beat up, his dorm ransacked, things missing."

There were other elements initially out of his parents' control. At age 15, Jeffrey became angry and destructive. Eventually—through signing and other communicative techniques—his family came to understand how Jeffrey ached for the opportunities enjoyed by his younger brother and sister, Jacob and Crystal: Friends. Freedom. The sweet gifts of speech and hearing.

Jeffrey has developed into an intriguing and beautiful person while at the Northeast Center. Upon meeting him, he immediately went for my left wrist. On a previous occasion, he did the same thing to Hope Network's CEO, Phil Weaver.

"He loves watches; he wants to see if you're wearing a watch," says his instructor, Tonya, who has embraced Jeffrey to such a degree that she involves him in her own family—at restaurants, malls and more.

Though Jeffrey has always tested negative for autistic traits that might explain his fetish for watches—along with tires and trucks and shoes—he exhibits all four from time to time. At any given moment, he might have a half-dozen watches in one of his front pockets.

Jeffrey at age nine with his parents Dale and Carol, sister Crystal, and brother Jacob

By his father's best estimate, Jeffrey has owned upwards of 100 timepieces. When I visited the family's 1870s farmhouse in Alto one recent Sunday while Jeffrey was visiting, he proudly pulled four or five watches from his pockets, including a stopwatch like you might use at a sporting event.

Jeffrey's other traits include a great sense of humor —"He's very funny," says Tonya—and incredible energy. The latter sometimes manifests itself in teasing people in his midst, something his family and the staff at the Northeast Center do their best to curtail.

They also try to minimize brief episodes when Jeffrey will scream. His family and the Center staff typically respond by signing for him to zipper his mouth.

Jeffrey has never really communicated what his outbursts mean.

It could be that he's courting attention. Or trying to emphasize a point.

Then again, maybe Jeffrey Richards, in his own unique way, is simply celebrating this: That he is.

■　■　■　■　■　■

JESSICA *medemar*

FROM INNOCENCE LOST,
TO A LIFE OF HOPE AND JOY

There are baby pictures galore, and photos of her as a tot and as a youngster, and then scrapbooks dedicated to her life as a young adult and now a married mother-to-be.

But there are barely any photographs of Jessica Medemar as a 12-year-old girl.

It's almost as though some overriding force were in place so as to not capture on film the pain and almost unspeakable horror of that year.

It's at that tender age when Jessica was raped by a former friend of her family's, and became pregnant as a result, she relates.

It's difficult to fathom, absorbing the woman she is today, a 26-year-old dynamo who has soared against all odds, and now counts herself employed as a proud member of the Hope Network family.

Jessica's story is unique to be sure, but also reflective of other Hope advocates who conquered their own brand of misery and found solace in overcoming challenges to ably serve Hope's legions of consumers.

In Jessica's case, she is grateful for her post at DART (Developmental Adolescent Residential Treatment program), where she serves kids with neurodevelopmental conditions.

Growing up with the Milings gave Jessica a sense of belonging

A 26-year-old dynamo who has soared against all odds, and now counts herself employed as a proud member of the Hope Network family.

But the road was paved with heartache and sorrow, beginning with the assault that would change her life and put her on a path seeking love and acceptance.

She found it in the loving home of a foster family led by Jeff and Barb Miling of Dorr, one of several stops Jessica made after undergoing an abortion that she did not fully comprehend as a scared and lonely pre-teen.

Jessica was born in California during the autumn of 1984, and lived a short time in Japan while her adoptive father served in the U.S. military. They eventually settled south of Grand Rapids, where her dad drove truck and mom worked in fast food. The couple divorced when Jessica was about 11.

A year later, Jessica remembers suffering abuse at the hands of a person tied to the family—someone she should have been able to trust. She eventually confided in a friend and was promptly removed from her home by protective services. She doesn't remember much of the abortion, and to this day wonders whether proper procedures and paperwork were in place when it occurred.

"I was completely alone," she remembers feeling. "I cried myself to sleep a few times. My brain did pretty well blocking out that time of my life."

Still, she felt denied, robbed of a significant part of her childhood. "I did have some good times, but most of it was not very fun. I had a really hard time trusting people. I pushed them way. I still do sometimes."

She lived a while in a group home, then a foster home where "I hated it; the other girls made me do all the work." She talked her caseworker into seeking another option, and landed in the tiny town of Dorr, located in southern Kent County.

Barb Miling sat her down to tacos at their first meeting, and Jessica devoured them—along with generous portions of the love emanating from Barb, the woman she now calls mom.

"She looked like a scared little rabbit," Barb Miling remembers of that day some 14 years ago. "And I remember she looked up at her caseworker that day and said, 'I'm not leaving.'"

And to this day, Jessica never really has.

Barb—along with husband Jeff, who made his living in the automotive industry until retiring recently—previously had taken in some eight other female youngsters over the years. They're licensed through D.A. Blodgett-St. John's Homes and Hope for Children." These days, the couple runs a vibrant daycare business for up to 12 kids.

Under the Milings' care, Jessica initially rebelled, sneaking out during the wee hours to meet with young men. "She'd slide out at three in the morning, and I'd track her down and yank these guys out of their cars," says Barb. "They looked like they'd seen a demon."

Little by little, Jessica learned her boundaries, and how to accept the Milings' love—not only from Barb and Jeff but all seven of their

A wedding celebration with the whole family

biological children—Jeffrey, Joey, Jesse, Joshua, Jordan, Jonathan and "little Jessica."

Together, the 10 of them camped the Upper Peninsula, fished the state's waters, visited Florida, attended Kentwood Community Church and took in family parties with the Milings' extended family.

While attending Wayland-Union High School, Jessica met Jared, two years her senior. Jessica stayed in the Miling home until she was 18, the same year she graduated Wayland, in 2003.

The next year, Jessica married the boy who'd taken her to the prom, and the couple now lives in Allegan County, about eight miles west of the Miling compound.

Jared works as a service manager for a tractor dealership. Jessica is just a few credits shy of an associate degree from Grand Rapids Community College.

It's a dramatic about-face for a woman who was in trauma as a young girl, and Hope Network is part of the formula now serving as a strong anchor in her life.

Jessica joined the DART program in the spring of 2007. When she learned she was pregnant, however, she transferred to another Hope program because of the high-risk nature of her job at DART, and currently serves older adults with Alzheimer's or other age-onset disabilities at the Side-by-Side program at Hope's Family Life Center on Grand Rapids' West Side. She'll return to DART after giving birth.

She's especially empathetic to the kids enrolled at DART: "Some of them have been abused, left behind, and I know how that feels."

Of the Milings' influence, Jessica says, "They gave me the family I should have had. They are my savior. They took me in, put up with all my crap, and would not let me push them away.

"They introduced me to God, and they introduce me to others as their daughter."

She knows she's surrounded now by people she can trust, people who love her and people to whom she can turn. Her husband. The Milings. The people with whom she works at Hope.

Barb Miling gazes into a color photograph of Jessica when she was just 2. She is wearing earrings given by her grandmother. She's dressed in striped bib overalls, seated on a parquet floor and smiling like an angel.

"I wish I would have got her then," says Barb, "before it all started."

She manages a smile. "Sounds greedy, doesn't it?"

■ ■ ■ ■ ■ ■

Courtesy Photo

25

OF PAYING DEBTS AND SECOND CHANCES

For some of us, the turning point in a life stems from something subtle.

For others, it's an event of incredible magnitude.

For Ben Rosa— who works with ex-offenders as a senior program manager for Hope Network's Workforce Development—it centered on the sum of $600.

"It's still painful for me to talk about it," says Ben, 59, remembering a day of some 18 years ago.

But he does, courageously so. Because if his story can inspire even one other person to circumvent the mistake he made, he figures it's worth telling.

Maybe it could sway a wayward kid.

Prevent someone from a life of crime.

Who knows; even save a life.

Ben was born in the U.S. territory of Puerto Rico, one of three boys raised by parents Ishmael and Ines. They moved to the mainland when Ben was about 8. "They wanted more," says Ben.

Initially, they settled in Chicago, but eventually followed an aunt to the Grand Rapids area. Ben attended Jefferson and Sigsbee Elementaries, then graduated in 1970 from Ottawa Hills High.

Four years later, he held a diploma in psychology from Central Michigan University, and after picking apples because full-time jobs were scarce, he volunteered his services with 61st District Court in Grand Rapids, working alongside probation officers.

He got his big break in 1975, when he signed on full-time as a bailiff, with his main function being the transfer of prisoners between their cells and court appearances.

He later was promoted to probation officer, and enjoyed working alongside cons and cops for nearly two decades.

Then, he got into a kind of trouble that virtually no one saw coming. Ben was convicted of misappropriating $600 while on the job, a felony.

In some circles, that might not sound like much. But because Ben had been elevated to a position of public trust, the presiding judge held him to a higher standard, and sentenced him to 2 to 4 years at the state prison in Jackson. He also was obliged to pay the money back. He resigned his job.

The motive behind his deed? Ben didn't need the money. He was married and had a steady income, a good life. "Pure greed," he says, "and believe me, greed is not a good thing."

He also blames his act on who he was at the time, how he perceived things: "The person I was 18 years ago is not the person I am now."

Another man might have reacted bitterly to the sentence he received, especially when you consider that Ben had had no prior criminal record.

But he took his medicine, to a point where he can now look back and say that being locked up was "probably the best thing that ever happened to me."

He ultimately served nine months behind bars, rubbing shoulders with men who had been convicted of murder, rape. At one point, he shared a bunk with an armed robber who was doing his third stint.

On his first day of freedom following time served, he says his wife welcomed him home with the words "I'm outta here."

If his story can inspire even one other person to circumvent the mistake he made, he figures it's worth telling.

Ben is top row, left, and with him are his parents in background (Ines and Ishmael), along with (front, left to right) niece Courtney, brother Joe and nephew Jason (1999)

27

"I didn't blame her," says Ben, who has remarried since. "It was a pretty traumatic thing to put her through."

He exited prison in June 1993. He had just a few dollars in his pocket, and a run-down halfway house on Monroe Avenue NW to call home.

He was lucky enough to secure a job digging graves by hand for a gentleman who owned a cemetery—and whose backhoe was on the fritz.

The backbreaking work paid just $4 an hour.

"But it paid for my tether," he says of the electronic ankle device he wore for 11 months, and whose cost he was expected to absorb as part of his year-long parole.

While others might have been humbled to the point of defeat, Ben had something profound to lean on. While incarcerated, he'd recommitted his life to Christ. And his ability to accept the terms of his punishment and put up with the humiliation and climb out of the bottom, he says, was "only through the grace of God."

"I don't push my Christian faith on anybody," he says. "But I am involved in a prison ministry program, and I'll go and talk to groups."

He moved from the cemetery job into a position as a temp worker at a West Michigan manufacturer, where "I did every lousy job the regulars didn't want to do."

It paid off, and he secured full-time employment there. He faced a layoff in 2002, but before his exit, managed to earn a master's degree in management from Cornerstone University.

Armed with better credentials, but still dragging around the stigma that goes with having been convicted of a felony, he applied for full-time employment at Hope Network. Hope answered by taking a risk, plugging him in as a case manager working with ex-offenders.

Since then, Ben has worked his way up to where he is today, in charge of a staff of 10 who labor hard to get ex-cons back in circulation with jobs, dignity and wind at their backs.

Given the winds of public sentiment, it's not always easy.

"These are the modern-day lepers," Ben says of the 500 men (just five percent of their clients are women) his department serves annually. "We have to try to break that rate of recidivism," he emphasizes, "and yet, two-thirds of employers don't want to hire them."

Against all odds, Ben and his charges work hard to strike relationships and build trust with area employers, convincing them it's worth the chance.

Some ex-offenders do fall short. But Ben would rather point to this statistic: That between 84 and 92 percent of those enrolled in two programs he helps supervise hold down jobs and create new lives.

Ben remembers when "ten years ago, you couldn't get five people in a room to talk about re-entry issues. Now, we've got several hundred people involved, all trying to change the community's outlook on ex-offenders."

Ben notes that his office is hardly soft on crime: "If people break the law, they should be held accountable. But once the person serves their time, they deserve a second chance. It's not a giveaway; they've earned that. And if you don't give them that second chance, they're going to go back to what they know.

"Hope Network," says Ben, "helps to break the cycle.

"And that's why I love our name…Hope!"

YOUNG LIVES
ON THE VERGE

HOPE'S LITTLE ANGEL—"MIRACLE MOLLIE"

Mollie Samuels is tearing up the back yard of her father's home on the outskirts of Big Rapids, running here and there, turning somersaults in a plastic bubble, monkeying her way up and down and all around a playset.

Not unusual for a healthy 4-year-old girl.

But Mollie is lucky to be alive, much less bouncing pell-mell, her arms and legs akimbo as she spreads her wings to inhale a world she was nearly denied.

"She was given a 1 percent chance of survival at birth," says Mollie's mother, Jamie Samuels, as she recounts the April day in 2007 when Mollie was delivered by emergency Caesarean section.

Her weight? Just 1 pound, 12 ounces. And she measured a tiny 12 inches in length.

"We were told that if she did live, to prepare for no chance of a normal life," says Jamie. "Some of the doctors predicted she'd be blind, deaf, have cerebral palsy."

But Mollie proved them all wrong, wringing out the first 11 months of her life in neonatal care at Spectrum Health Butterworth Hospital in downtown Grand Rapids.

Today, says Jamie, one of the doctors who attended to Mollie refers to her as "The Legend," a moniker assigned for her extraordinary pluck and will to fight against all odds.

"She is," says Jamie, "our Miracle Mollie."

he says. "That helped keep her alive, but it also keeps us on our toes." Part of the ongoing struggle is helping Mollie understand that she's no longer sick and can't be coddled.

"She needs rules and boundaries," says Jamie. "It's a delicate balance."

Though Mollie's parents never married and live apart, they're both in Big Rapids and they're both in her life. "When you've faced a life-and-death situation," explains Jamie, 30, "you parent together. We've experienced something incredible together, and we're grateful together."

Jamie has another daughter by another relationship, Harley, age 10, and her pregnancy with that child was normal.

One of Hope Network's youngest consumers, Mollie was first assessed at age 3 by staff at Hope Network Rehabilitation Services' outpatient clinic in Big Rapids, which serves a variety of diagnoses through comprehensive therapy programs. In essence, she went there to learn how to eat, since from birth, she'd been receiving nutrients via a "G tube" that leads through her abdomen into her stomach. It's still a struggle, and Mollie continues to work closely with Gayle Daugherty, a speech and language pathologist at the Big Rapids site, on the oral aversions she has to placing things in her mouth—everything from food and drink to a toothbrush.

Mollie's strengths, explains her father, Nick Kuiper, 29, are also roadblocks to progress. "She's an extremely strong-willed individual,"

"Our story isn't one of sadness,"
says Mollie's mother. "It's one of hope."

Courtesy Photos

Problems carrying Mollie, however, surfaced early. Jamie was already confined to bed rest when complications arose. Her water broke at 25 weeks, and an ultrasound confirmed she'd lost her amniotic fluid. Jamie was rushed by ambulance from Big Rapids to Spectrum, where she gave birth on April 16, 2007. "She looked lifeless," Jamie remembers of her first look at Mollie. "So teeny-tiny."

Along with a feeding tube, Mollie also underwent a tracheotomy, and relied on a ventilator for breathing from her birth up until just recently. Her tracheotomy was removed about two weeks ago, and reconstructive surgery to disguise the scar will likely occur early next year.

"We've lived one day at a time for four years," says Nick, "so we can wait another six months or so for that surgery."

In the meantime, Nick, who instructs in TV and digital media production at Ferris State University, and Jamie, who works as office manager and instructor at Rhythmic Sky Dance Studio in Big Rapids, continue to enjoy their relationship with Hope Network. They're especially grateful for the fact they don't have to travel often to Grand Rapids, a trip with which they became only too familiar during Mollie's first year. "We worried about what a small town would have to offer," says Jamie, "but the moment we walked into Hope Network here and met Gayle, it was a perfect fit. And we wouldn't have to exhaust ourselves of time and money" in making the 90-mile round trips to Grand Rapids.

With Gayle's guidance, Nick and Jamie do their best to have Mollie ingest a small meal six times daily. Both parents laud "Miss Gayle" for creating ingenious methods to make that happen, including the offer of simple rewards for a job well done. Mollie also has "homework" to complete between sessions, and is becoming more motivated all the time to earn praise. "She's made more progress with Hope Network than other programs we've tried," says Jamie.

If Jamie and Nick seem to have a healthy handle on their daughter's care, it's partly tied to Nick's decision four years ago to chronicle Mollie's life on tape. Since her birth, he's documented virtually every high moment and hurdle. Initially, the compact disc he produced served as the centerpiece for his thesis toward earning a master's degree in broadcast and cinematic arts from Central Michigan University.

But his work has also attracted a larger audience—the Public Broadcasting System—and already, a trio of PBS stations, one as far away as Kentucky, have committed to airing the 57-minute documentary. The other two are WCMU in Mt. Pleasant and WGVU serving the Grand Rapids area.

Nick's work is entitled "Preemie," and it features not only Mollie, but the stories of two other babies born prematurely who received care at Spectrum.

Jamie and Nick look back and realize how "we were so uneducated and unprepared" to deal with Mollie's birth, which they say was initially "traumatic and devastating."

Since then, though, they've grown to understand that "We've been blessed enough and made strong enough to be able to deal with it," says Jamie. "Our mission now is to educate others," she says, noting that she and Nick have served as spokespersons for the March of Dimes.

"It's not the end of the world," Jamie says of giving birth to a baby with special needs. "And our story isn't one of sadness.

"It's one of hope."

Mollie is all smiles when she's with her mom and dad

HOPE NETWORK HELPS HIGH SCHOOL STUDENT WEATHER STORMY SEAS

When Hope Network workers in the small town of Paris, MI arrived for work one recent day, they discovered a message in a bottle.

It hadn't been tossed from a deserted isle, nor did it bob for countless days atop windswept whitecaps.

But in a sense, it did bear the marks of a potential castaway. And it expressed all the bittersweet angst of being launched into new and untested waters.

Michael VanPortliet authored the note and sealed it in a jar after completing three years of intense training at an enterprise for at-risk high school students in Paris known as the "Leader Program."

Designed for students who don't take to traditional teaching methods at a trio of high schools in Mecosta and Osceola Counties, the Leader Program works in concert with those schools to provide vocational training in a factory-like atmosphere where the real world rules.

One needs only to grasp the sheer poetry in Michael's letter to be convinced that for him, the program took—and in big ways.

"Michael has a willingness to help others, an ability to be self-supervised, and the gifts to be a model and a leader for others," says Amy Kienitz, a site supervisor at the Paris campus.

Michael with the Hope Network team (left to right): Site Supervisor Amy Kienitz; Senior Manager Betsye Anderson; Teacher and Site Supervisor Lonnie Day and Site Coordinator Randie Hatchew

Michael VanPortliet "has turned it around completely."
—Randie Hatchew

Adds Lonnie Day, a certified teacher and site supervisor, "Michael worked hard, kept me entertained, and led the group."

That's high praise for a young man of 19 who, just a few years ago, nearly dropped out of high school, and courted a life of, well, who knows what?

Instead—thanks in part to job training and more that he secured in Paris—Michael not only earned his diploma, but now holds down a full-time job with benefits at an industrial washing facility, a startling transformation from the person he was a short time ago.

"This gave me guidance," he says of the Hope Network team that helped him hone interview skills, build a resume and perform production work quickly and efficiently.

37

"If it weren't for them, I'd probably be jobless right now. And I used to run with a rough crowd."

Not anymore, though, largely on account of what he's learned about personal responsibility, and a desire to set himself up for a future that he hopes will include a home of his own and increased job opportunities.

It also helps that he needs to rise pretty early from his bed in the nearby town of Morley to make it to his job in Grand Rapids that begins each weekday at 6 a.m. It's an hour commute each way.

Michael is proud of his accomplishments, but hardly one to broadcast them. In fact, his humility is almost overwhelming.

"They are proud of me," he says of people in his midst who have seen him soar. "But I try not to think too highly of myself."

Instead, he's extolling others who have made an impact in his life, the Hope Network team among them.

"A lot of people have really big egos," says Betsye Anderson, senior manager in Paris. "Michael is definitely humble."

And at an age when a fairly significant number of his peers might be chasing wants rather than needs, Michael keeps it simple.

"With a little water and a little food," he says, "more than likely we'll see the next day."

Michael is prone to profundity perhaps because he takes his time in choosing his words—sometimes LOTS of time.

Hope Network Senior Manager Betsye Anderson pushed Michael to set goals and dream big

During his interview with CAKE, it wasn't unusual for him to mull a question for 10 or even 20 seconds before answering.

That sort of attention to detail and an affinity to express himself succinctly has had a dramatic effect on Hope Network staff.

"He's turned it around completely," says Randie Hatchew, a site coordinator. "From the very first time I met Michael, he's come around 100 percent to be a strong hard worker with a great personality."

Betsye Anderson goes so far as to say that Michael—and specifically, the letter he put in a bottle and left for staff—helped her re-commit to the 20 years she's already put in at Hope.

"That letter is one of those things that keeps me grounded, that keeps me here," she says.

"Just when I think I want to explore some other professions, well, when I read that letter, it helped remind me once more that what we do at Hope Network is so much more than just collecting a check."

■ ■ ■ ■ ■ ■

INSIDE THE LETTER: "I LOVED IT HERE"

After Michael VanPortliet concluded his formal vocational training with Hope Network of Paris this past June, he drove home and had a strawberry swirl ice cream cone with his mother, Teresa, in the family kitchen.

He was sad, and Teresa knew it, and she consoled him by reminding him that the job he'd start that week meant a fresh beginning.

"She's very wise," Michael said of his mom.

Still, he retreated to his bedroom.

And he cried.

"I cried a lot," he acknowledges. "I wasn't looking forward to this (formal relationship with Hope Network) ending. I wanted to keep it going."

He found solace in a pad of paper and a pen. And spent the next four hours refining a note that would serve as a thank-you and a goodbye.

"I tried to think of everything that I wanted to say to a lot of people. I wanted them to know that I loved it here."

The letter done, he placed it into jar, screwed on the top, and drove back to Hope Network. It was after midnight, the place closed up and empty.

He went around to the break area out back, sat on the picnic table, smoked a Marlboro, and into the dark, whispered "Well, I'm gonna miss you."

Then he put his message in the bottle at the entrance to the place he'd known as his second home, a place where he was always welcome, always belonged. Always will.

Kevin Chilton turned the Project Search experience into a full-time job

PROJECT SEARCH—TRANSITIONING HIGH SCHOOL STUDENTS INTO THE REAL WORLD

When Kevin Chilton showed up at a summertime picnic in a suit and tie, someone reminded him that it was "just a picnic."

But Kevin was in the hunt for a job, and doing everything in his power to impress. His response to "just a picnic?"

"There is no '*just*.'"

Today, 22-year-old Kevin is working in the commercial loans department at Fifth Third Bank's Corporate Service Center on East Paris Avenue in southeast Grand Rapids. And he owes it in part to a program called "Project Search" that helped him develop job skills not merely from books, but by actually showing up.

Across town, at Spectrum Health's Butterworth campus, Abbie Friskey, 18, is poised to accept a part-time post there—again, thanks to her involvement in Project Search, which helps her live out what it's like to work in a hospital.

"This is a program that opens up the door for that student who needs a little extra help," says James Ritsema, a paraprofessional with the program. "It gets them job-ready, and out into the real world."

Project Search is an employer-based internship program that relies on four key groups of players—Hope Network, Grand Rapids Public Schools, Michigan Rehabilitation Services as the primary

Carlos Gober

Abbie Friskey

Kyle Winters

funding agency, and employers like Fifth Third and Spectrum Health.

Together, they're creating innovative ways to provide an edge for employable high school seniors from Kent County schools who have mental or physical challenges. In essence, Project Search serves as their final year of secondary schooling.

"The goal is to get these students a job—to keep them off public assistance," says Lisa Erhan, a teacher from Grand Rapids Public Schools based at Spectrum. "It's every parent's dream, to have kids who are productive members of society. And it's not just training, but employment that we're after."

Cari Brooks works for Hope Network as a job coach with the program. "These kids have done amazing jobs," she says. "They're truly becoming professionals. And they're immersed in community settings. It's truly amazing to see their progress."

It's Cari's job to work side-by-side with the other professionals, and she's responsible for helping teach the interns a wide variety of skills: how to dress and use appropriate language, the proper social skills to maintain, how to work quickly and efficiently, how to accept feedback, and also how to build a resume, fill out applications and interview for a job.

The program is intense.

Students sign on for an entire school year. They must arrange transportation to either Fifth Third or Spectrum, and excuses for being late or absent aren't tolerated. Some spend as much as two hours on buses each way.

Students assigned to Spectrum rub shoulders with doctors, nurses and patients

Kim Stone

A typical day begins at 8:30 a.m. with 90 minutes of instruction, followed by a workday at any one of several stations until 3 p.m.

It's not all feet up on the desk and lolling about the water cooler. Just ask Brittany O'Conner, 20, of Ottawa Hills High, who mans a desk most afternoons in a job that is alternately rigorous, routine and rewarding.

Someday, Brittany would like to work as a photographer or wedding planner or animae creator. But for now, she's committed to Project Search, realizing how it's helping her lay a solid foundation for dreams deferred.

Same goes for Susan Geelhoed, 19, of Grand Rapids Christian High, who stuffs envelopes as part of her job at Fifth Third. She smiles. "Paper cuts? I got plenty," and she holds up her fingers.

But Susan shows up day after day because she understands the value. Her teacher, Grand Rapids Public School instructor Karl Schantz, calls Susan "one of our most punctual, very reliable."

Carlos Gober is up every day at 6 a.m. to make it to Fifth Third. "I like my job," he says, and Schantz is quick to point out how Carlos is "efficient, accurate and fast." So much so that, like Abbie and Kevin, he may be in line for a paying job here someday.

While most the stations at Fifth Third are of a clerical nature, students assigned to Spectrum rub shoulders with doctors, nurses, patients—and the attendant drama and trauma that can surface.

Abbie, a Kenowa Hills senior, spends part of every day accommodating families waiting for loved ones to emerge from surgery. It's not for everyone, requiring both aplomb and sensitivity, qualities she's learned on the job. She dreams of becoming a licensed practical nurse. Of her role now, she says "This is preparing me for a real job, a real life."

Alicia Rzepka, 19, who hails from Cedar Springs High, stocks patient rooms at Helen DeVos Children's Hospital. She's in and out of sick kids' quarters, and has learned to be discreet, conscientious. She loves being in the presence of nurses, and plans to become a certified nursing assistant. "I go home feeling good," she says of her workdays.

Not everyone is going to immediately transition into a job where they've spent a school year. But Kevin Chilton is the exception; he's graduated Project Search and now works as a full-time employee at Fifth Third. He's got his eyes on a management position, and if a suit and tie helps, he's ready to don it again.

"This was my pathway," he says of Project Search, now in its third year at the bank. "Society sometimes overlooks certain skill sets, and if you're given the opportunity like I was, you can contribute as much as someone who's taken college classes."

Terri Larsen, a human resources specialist at Fifth Third, says students like Kevin and the others "make us a better place to work," adding, "We learn something from these interns every day."

Kyle Winters, 26, of Rockford, works in Spectrum's Post-Anesthetic Care Unit—where patients come to after surgery and other procedures. He fills ice packs, stocks blankets, even transports patients on gurneys throughout the hospital.

His daily goal isn't just something reinforced by his Project Search teachers; it was suggested a long time ago by his grandfather, Tom Lannon. "Every time I see my grandpa," says Kyle, "he asks me, 'Did you bring joy into someone's life today?'"

Kyle grins. "I do."

Susan Geelhoed

KEEPING PROJECT SEARCH ALIVE AND WELL

It's no secret that funding for education is a rollercoaster ride. That concerns advocates for Project Search, which relies on a combination of resources—funds from Michigan Rehabilitation Services and agencies like the Grand Rapids Community Foundation, employees supplied by Grand Rapids Public Schools, coaches and supervisors affiliated with Hope Network, and private contributions.

"This is such a valuable program," says Lisa Erhan, a teacher with GRPS who works with students assigned to Spectrum Health. "Out of all the programs I've been with in my 22 years as an educator, this is the one most geared toward getting students employed, rather than just teaching them skills."

Adds Anne Schefke, an occupational therapist with Project Search: "This program is what school is all about, getting these students employment."

Project Search was founded some 15 years ago in Ohio, when a supervisor at a children's hospital in Cincinnati became frustrated with the high turnover rate in entry-level jobs involving the re-stocking of supplies. Leaning on multiple collaborations, Project Search was born, and has since spread to more than 150 sites in 40-plus states and four countries.

In Michigan, the program thrives with Hope Network's participation not only in Kent County, but at Mercy Memorial Hospital System in Monroe, with collaboration from the Monroe County Intermediate School District.

As many as 12 students are enrolled per site, and rotate to different stations every 10 weeks or so, building new skill sets as they progress through the program.

Project Search is always looking for ways to grow, and for advocates to give of their time, talents and treasures.

For more information on how you might contribute, contact Hope Network's Cindy Alferink, Project Search Coordinator, at (616) 464-1176, or at: CAlferink@hopenetwork.org

HOPE FROM THE INSIDE OUT

"SHINING A LIGHT" ON HOPE NETWORK BOARD MEMBER JOHN VANDER PLOEG AND HIS PASSION FOR HELPING OTHERS

One of the most beloved and respected members of the Hope Network family earned his first dollar at age 10, pulling weeds from among radishes and onions on a "truck farm" near Lansing, Ill.

It paid exactly 27 and a half cents per hour, and John Vander Ploeg proudly recalls showing off his first weekly paycheck for $11 to his mother. John had every intention of buying a bicycle with his cash—and soon—until his mother sat him down and shared with her son that the first 10 percent of his money would always go to the church.

"Who made up that rule?" little Johnny asked.

He then learned that after waving goodbye to a buck and change, an even heftier portion would be socked into savings, since all five Vander Ploeg children were responsible for paying toward their Christian education.

"What I soon came to realize," John Vander Ploeg says 66 years later from his home in Portage, "was that it was going to take me a lot longer to get that bike than I thought."

Those early lessons about giving and getting have served John Vander Ploeg well.

"One of those people I can always call on."
—Phil Weaver describing Vander Ploeg

John (center) helping women from Kenya secure jobs

Today, as a long-standing member of Hope Network's Board of Directors and its Foundation Board, John has brought a wealth of wisdom and grace to an organization that depends on savvy leadership to guide it into the future.

"He's one of those guys who makes us better," says Hope CEO Phil Weaver, "and quite frankly, makes me a better person.

"John has a passion for helping people. There's no façade. He genuinely cares, and he makes a big difference in people's lives."

Like his colleagues on the board, John is comfortable letting Hope's employees and consumers largely take the public credit for Hope Network's success. But in the background, those trustees wrestle with complex issues that affect the organization in ways big and small—no easy task given the state of flux that rules our economy in general, and health care in particular.

Though John commands a position of power and influence and trust in more ways than one these days, he came from humble beginnings, the son of a Christian Reformed Church (CRC) pastor for who the first nine years of his career drew no salary, satisfied to live off what was left over from Sunday collections that paid the church bills.

Playing golf for Hope Network (left to right):
Dick Dalke, Mike Vander Ploeg, Mel Klooster and
John Vander Ploeg

John was born in Grand Rapids, where his father first served East Paris CRC in Kentwood from 1930 until 1939. Young John was just 4 when the family moved to Pella, Iowa, and remembers their 1934 Ford dying on the road just five miles from the parsonage.

A farmer and his tractor towed them into town, where the church council president—who owned a Chevy dealership—suggested to John's dad that because he now would indeed be paid a salary, he could afford $10 a month toward a new car.

"The next morning," says John, "we had a brand new '39 Chevy, and I think it cost us $700."

Six years later, the Vander Ploegs moved to Lansing, Ill., just south of Chicago, where they stayed five years. John was halfway through high school when the family moved again, this time to Kalamazoo.

John graduated from Kalamazoo Christian High, then attended Calvin College and Western Michigan University. He married Margaret Mejeur when they were both 20 and both worked for a rubber stamp company.

Their first date? A roller-skating party.

John sold packaging supplies for the first 10 years they were married, but was convinced there was a large and lucrative market for sophisticated industrial packaging.

In 1964, he and Margaret—proud parents of a 1-month-old-son—both quit their jobs and begged $1,000 each from seven friends, then used the $7,000 to establish their own business.

It grew slowly at first, from a fledgling storefront enterprise that comprised just 800 square feet. Margaret's mother, whom they affectionately referred to as "Ma," took care of their newborn in her home just down the street while both parents minded the store. "We would have never pulled it off if it weren't for her," says John, who watched in awe as their enterprise, "Ship-Pac Inc." grew into a multi-million dollar success.

John with his wife, Margaret, at their home in Portage, Michigan

Even while their business flourished, the couple became active in politics, Christian education, church affairs and social reform.

The Vander Ploegs are no strangers to travel or sacrifice, having made untold trips overseas on behalf of the Christian Reformed World Relief Committee (CRWRC) to perform disaster and recovery work.

It's while serving 15 years as a board member with CRWRC that John met Herb Start and Jim Tuinstra, who were both active with that organization before going forward to help establish Hope Network.

John, then, became intimately involved with Hope from the very start, and has been one of its strongest supporters for decades.

"I see the opportunity to do what the Lord told us to do—imitate Jesus Christ," John says of his commitment to Hope. "And I just enjoy it. It's a terrific board with amazing talent—people committed to the mission who have the special skill sets to achieve what they believe in."

Adds Phil Weaver: "John is one of the people I can always call on, and whatever the situation. I'll ask him if he can make himself available for, say, next Tuesday, and it's always 'Oh, I'd love to.' "He's just so positive about assisting our organization."

John was grateful for the chance recently to see Hope Network from a fairly different perspective—watching as a friend received services for a brain aneurysm that nearly killed him. "The change in that man was amazing," John says of the way Hope's Transitional Living Program rehabilitated him. "Most people would never know that he ever had a serious problem."

In addition to working tirelessly for Hope Network, John has played an active role in Kalamazoo Christian Schools. He was named Michigan Small Businessman of the Year in 1982. He has served on nearly a dozen community boards, and as a councilman for the City of Kalamazoo, served the city as vice-mayor for four years.

John and Margaret also give of their time and resources to help people who might not be directly associated with one of the many organizations with which they're affiliated, but are in dire need. They recently went to great pains to provide $500 to a family in Kenya that lives in squalor. Asked to elaborate on why the couple gives so generously, he says, "We can and we should and we must."

Of his roles at Hope Network, John puts everything in God's hands. "A lot of the time, I'll just pray for Him to give me the right words, the right skills. 'You need to be in charge,' I'll say, and I lay it on the Lord. 'You put me in this place with this opportunity; now what do I do?'"

John believes that Christians have a responsibility to share their faith with others: "Each of us needs to let our light shine," he says. "And I see Hope Network as helping shine that light in a magnificent way."

■ ■ ■ ■ ■ ■

TEN THINGS THAT MAKE JOHN VANDER PLOEG SPECIAL!

1. He's usually reading two books at a time. Loves whodunits, history and politics.

2. Daughter Kathie, who now directs Ship-Pac, is married to Andy Hoekstra, brother of former U.S. Rep. Pete Hoekstra.

3. Guilty pleasure? Ice cream.

4. What he doesn't brag about but could: His past life as a racquetball player. For some 30 years, he played regularly from 6-7 a.m.

5. "You ain't much if you ain't Dutch!" And for proof, he and Margaret have kissing Dutch statuary in their front yard, plus a miniature windmill just off the side patio.

6. John's father once served as editor of "The Banner," a monthly publication of the Christian Reformed Church.

7. What he most often prays for? "Thy will be done."

8. Country he'd most like to re-visit? Switzerland.

9. How you learn patience? Following an injury years ago, John spent four months in a cast that reached from his neck to his hips.

10. In his scant spare time, John loves to cook. His specialty? Drunken chicken!

JUNE SMITH'S CALLING CARD?
MORE THAN WHAT A GARDEN GROWS

When June Smith comes calling with her potting soil and seedlings, it's love that blooms alongside the blossoms.

For more than 20 years, June has been cultivating not only flower beds, but friends, as she works her green thumb among Hope Network consumers, helping them to see reflections of themselves in little miracles of growth, the turning of seasons.

June's role as gardener was a circuitous one. She was born and raised on a farm in Eaton Rapids, graduating from the high school there in 1945.

She enrolled at St. Lawrence School of Nursing in Lansing, but after losing a kidney, quit partway through. She landed a job in a doctor's office, married, had three children with husband Bob, and eventually moved to the Grand Rapids area.

At 40, she lost the sight in her right eye, an effect, doctors said, of the kidney she'd lost. She was told she only had a few years left to live.

That was 44 years ago.

Undaunted, she enrolled at Grand Rapids Junior College, where she earned an associate degree. She was tapped to help develop the Forest Hills school system, and came to appreciate all things education.

"I discovered that I loved it, and so I went to MSU, and later Western Michigan, where I earned my certification as a teacher."

She taught earth science at a junior high in Wyoming, then traveled with Bob to a job he landed in Iran, and taught at a private school in Tehran that boasted students from 52 countries. "What a joy," she says. "I definitely learned more than they did."

June says you might be surprised at what her overseas pupils craved more than almost anything else: "Homework!" she exclaims.

Upon returning to the States, June taught again for Wyoming Public Schools, but this time as a special education instructor for grades 1 through 3.

She says she specialized in giving hugs, and that's easy to see, given the way in which she interacts today with Hope Network residents.

"I give lots of hugs and kisses," says June, "because staff can't always do that."

June's impact runs deep at a handful of Hope programs—Side By Side, Wildwood, Sojourners and Maplewood, to name just a few. Volunteering is a natural outgrowth of an experience she enjoyed while earning her Master Gardener certificate from the MSU Extension Service following her years as a schoolteacher.

"The Master Gardening class requires 40 hours of volunteer work," June explains, "and I did mine at the Michigan Christian Home."

Even though she was retired from teaching, she saw the opportunity to help others as a new career path, and one with spiritual connections.

"I have always felt that God had a purpose in everything I've done," she says, and that includes a six-month backpacking trip

June Smith's recipe for success?
"To find the best in others."

51

around the world that she and Bob embarked on after she left the classroom in 1987.

She found her way to Hope Network 21 years ago, and has been working with groups of consumers ever since to create flower beds, square-foot vegetable gardens, patio gardens and even indoor experiments.

How does your garden grow?
With lots of hugs.

She's also famous for the garden parties she hosts for Hope at her own home—complete with a smorgasbord that includes barbequed chicken legs, coleslaw, cheesy potatoes, fresh fruit and pineapple upside-down cake.

Last week at Wildwood, June held court for about a dozen consumers eager to nurture fledgling tomato plants. Gingerly, she helped her crew transplant seedlings from small containers into large pots that would encourage growth.

"You need a lot more dirt in there, honey," she said to one, and then to them all, "Remember guys, you may not have to diaper these plants, but you do need to feed 'em. And water, too."

Her time spent on Hope campuses is appreciated by more than residents: "She's been coming here a long time, and everyone appreciates it," says April Capps, an independent lead instructor at Wildwood.

June has also earned the admiration and respect of the Hope family for gifts found in pots and planters: "She brings out the best in people," says Lisa McCready, a recreation assistant.

"She's very genuine, and what I love about her is her love of life. She's very inspirational, and an example of how we should all live our lives."

June turns the compliments back on Hope's consumers and staff: "The joy that I get from these guys is much more than what I get," she says.

"I love 'em all."

A MEASURE OF SUCCESS

Everyone can participate in the gardening fun.

Of all the things June Smith keeps in her handbag, this rarely leaves it, a little essay by Ralph Waldo Emerson:

"What Is Success?"

To laugh often and much;

To win the respect of intelligent people and the affection of children;

To earn the appreciation of honest critics and endure the betrayal of false friends;

To appreciate beauty; to find the best in others;

To leave the world a bit better, whether by a healthy child, a garden patch or a redeemed social condition;

To know even one life has breathed easier because you have lived.

THE WHEELS ON THE BUSES GO 'ROUND AND 'ROUND (BOY, DO THEY EVER!)

Few things say "Hope Network" like the iconic red and white buses that buzz about Kent County and environs.

But far more important than the vehicles themselves is the precious cargo within.

Just ask Matt DeBose.

Or his brother Clarence.

Or any of the other 45 men and women who jump into the driver's seat day in and day out to provide more than a quarter-million rides annually for the some 2,000 consumers who depend on Hope's Department of Transportation Services.

"Some of our drivers are on the road 12 hours a day, and if there's snow, 15," says Joan Konyndyk, director of transportation services, emphasizing that drivers take breaks for safety's sake.

The DeBose brothers both forged careers at Steelcase, Inc., before deciding to spend their retirement years in the service of others.

Matt, who's the older of the two siblings at 72, considered putting in for a job with an area school system after his 19 years at Steelcase. But during his first exposure to Hope's consumers, he was hooked. "If you want somebody to appreciate you," he says of passengers on his bus, "they really appreciate you."

*Joan Konyndyk, Director of Transportation Services,
with Matt DeBose and Clarence DeBose*

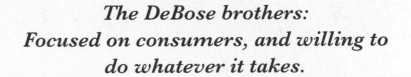

**The DeBose brothers:
Focused on consumers, and willing to
do whatever it takes.**

Clarence, who's 68, remembers walking out the doors of Steelcase after 21 years and "walking into a different world" at Hope Network.

"I said 'Wow!' These are people who really need me. There'd have to be something really, really wrong for me to stop doing what I'm doing."

The DeBose brothers hail from a family of 10 children born to a father who worked as a pastor, and his homemaker wife. From time to time, the couple took in foster children—some with special needs—which meant living in close quarters in the home on Grand Rapids' South Side.

"And miles to go before I sleep…"

Both brothers worked a variety of odd jobs during their youth—everything from delivering the Grand Rapids Herald to washing cars. Both graduated from the now-defunct South High School, and eventually signed on at the office furniture giant.

Matt came on board first with Hope, in 2002. Clarence followed a few years later. They both work shifts of at least 30 hours weekly, and have come to know virtually all the myriad routes that crisscross Grand Rapids and surrounding communities. Clarence has a regular route most days, while Matt bats utility for drivers in need of a sub.

Joan Konyndyk can't say enough about them: "They're very dedicated. I never have to worry about either one showing up."

In fact, there's probably more concern that the brothers don't overdo. According to Transportation Services Manager Al Wiltse, Matt walked in after a 10-hour shift recently, only to find out that another driver coming into work had suddenly learned that her daughter had been taken to a hospital following a car accident.

"Matt turned right around," Al remembers. "Didn't even punch out. Just went right back out again. Probably did another three hours."

Al says that both brothers—and this is reflective of the nearly four dozen others who drive as well—take their positions very seriously.

"They're really focused on the consumers," he says, "and willing to do whatever it takes."

Both brothers have tender stories to tell about the special way they've been inspired by certain passengers.

Matt recalls the first time he picked up a consumer who could neither walk nor talk, and had a hard time moving his legs and arms. "It's all I could do from breaking down in tears," he says.

■ ■ ■ ■ ■ ■

ALL ABOARD BUS NO. 79

It's 1:30 p.m. when we pull out of the parking lot on 36th Street SE, where the fleet is parked and maintained. The first stop is just 100 yards away, in Building 1 on the same campus, where Clarence waits for a consumer to be bundled up against the cold.

He patiently walks beside her as she shuffles slowly to the bus. He guides her up the steps, one arm around her waist. Once she's in and he's at the wheel of the bus, he glances back: "You buckled up, babe?"

Click.

"Alright!" says Clarence, and pulls away.

We travel east on 36th and then south on Kalamazoo to drop off our young lady in the Crystal Springs development, then pick up five more consumers at an area business not far from there.

It's a fairly lively handful of men and women, and it includes two male passengers who tease each other about what should be the hot topic of conversation—one sticks to sports, while the other would rather discuss world events. Eventually, talk revolves around Clarence. In short, they feel comfortable and safe with him as their driver. They like him, and they say so.

Clarence is en route back to the 36th Street campus, but needs to drop off Leetrice Souza first at a home on the city's South Side. Before she exits, though, Leetrice relates how Clarence provides her with sweet freedom. Then she delivers the quote of the day:

"My grandma's like, 'You get out more than I do!'"

Clarence helps a consumer board the bus

FOR ALL THE RIGHT REASONS: RON QUAKKELAAR'S PARTNERSHIP WITH HOPE INSPIRES OTHERS TO GIVE

So there he was, a young man of maybe 18 or 19, slopping floors and cleaning toilets and dumping trash at a place called Pine Rest, when all of a sudden, he had this epiphany. It didn't originate from the tile he was scrubbing or the gunk he was responsible for removing, though.

His turning point was cast by the sight of a little kid's head bobbing within a safety helmet. A child he'd catch chewing on the cord that powered the buffing machine. Some little girl whose eyes were stuck in space.

And it was during those moments when Ron Quakkelaar realized how blessed he was, and that part of his destiny should be to share whatever came his way. Today, tomorrow, always.

"That's when my eyes opened up," Ron was recalling. "Even back then when I was working hard and working long hours, I remember telling myself, 'Man, you got a lot to be thankful for.'"

A 1973 graduate of South Christian High School, Ron would go on to earn degrees from Grand Rapids Junior College and Western Michigan University. After graduating, he secured an accounting job with a gravel company, doubling as their dispatcher, staying 10 years.

Hope's annual golf outing (left to right): Bill Battjes, Construction Manager at Hope Network, Ron Quakkelaar, Dan Holbert, Hope Network Chief Administration Officer, and Todd Zaccanelli, Ron's invited guest and owner of Pete's Grill in Byron Center

But he never forgot the image of those kids, of youngsters in need. And when he signed on with Dykhouse Construction in 1989, it provided ample opportunities to partner with a non-profit looking for a helping hand.

Ron Quakkelaar, meet Hope Network.

Or more specific to Ron's case, meet Mary Kloster, Hope's Director of Housing.

Dykhouse Construction had already cemented a relationship with Hope prior to Ron's arrival, but it was Mary's persuasive nature that prompted Ron to amp up his involvement with the organization.

"I'd worked with Hope's different regimes over the years, but Mary had this presence," says Ron with a smile.

Sharing what comes his way...
today, tomorrow, always...

59

"And she said to me, 'Ron, you should be a sponsor of our annual walk.'"

Ron said OK, and the next thing he knew, was soliciting donations from subcontractors who helped Dykhouse build everything from bungalows to banks. Ron and friends have since turned in more than $65,000 via the runs. And thanks to some more gentle arm-twisting, Dykhouse Construction, where Ron now serves as major owner, is title sponsor of Hope's annual golf outing at Egypt Valley Country Club.

"I think the best way to describe Ron is a businessman with a heart," says Mary, who's been on board with Hope for nearly two decades. "Other owners of companies might be a little disconnected. But Ron isn't that way at all. And that's what makes him and his company unusual."

While Ron's happy to raise funds for Hope, he's a whole lot more uncomfortable touting his business in the process, and was actually embarrassed to see a banner fluttering in the breeze at the country club, ballyhooing the Dykhouse name. "I got a little ribbing from the guys," he acknowledges.

But in the same breath, Ron understands that sometimes you have to put your name and your reputation out there so others might be inspired to give. It's the only reason, in fact, that he agreed to be featured in The Book of CAKE.

Case in point: After each of Hope's annual runs, it's customary to recognize the party who raised the most money. "He never wants to be included in that," Mary emphasizes. "He's not in it for the recognition." Ron developed

his life's mantra—"Do unto others" from two elements: A close tie to his religion, and the realization that hard work never hurt anyone.

At the tender age of 11, he was already serving his bricklayer father as a tender, which is to say that he mixed the mortar and kept it coming for the guy with the trowel. "I still remember him saying, 'Now don't make it too watery!'

"I don't mean to brag," says Ron, "but I had to work for everything. I played sports in high school, but every Saturday, I'd help lay those bricks. It wasn't long before I knew this wasn't what I wanted to do for the rest of my life."

It was while he was enrolled at junior college that he scored a job at Pine Rest, of which Hope Network used to be a part. "I would work the children's retreat," says Ron, and that's especially where he observed kids with physical, mental and emotional concerns.

He was never able to shake the thought of how some of them suffered so, and when he became major owner at Dykhouse, he didn't need to have his arm bent much for the sake of them and others like them.

In recent years, Ron and his company have built, remodeled or repaired more than two dozen Hope properties that house everything from office space to rehab quarters. In fact, there's hardly a Hope site Ron himself hasn't personally visited.

His commitment to engage himself personally is perhaps best told by the degree to which he went to perform work at a Hope facility in Flint. (See related story).

Blueprints find a home

60

And he's not afraid to get his own hands dirty, either. Over the years, Ron himself has pitched in on projects as large as constructing a new building, but he's also helped repair drywall, replace doors, paint a gazebo, put up fencing—you name it. "He'll do anything he can," says Mary, "big or small."

Working on so many Hope Network sites puts Ron face to face with folks who benefit directly from the organization's outreach, and he often wanders back to another time and place where those kids made their impact and inspired him to lend a helping hand.

"If people could see what I see," says Ron, "Hope would never be short of contributions."

Converting those observations into action is Hope's gain—again and again. "He's in it for all the right reasons," Mary says of Ron's involvement. "And that's what all of us appreciate the most."

■ ■ ■ ■ ■ ■ ■

Ron and Bill Battjes enjoy a moment with Phil Weaver at Hope Network's Legacy Gala

THE LENGTHS TO WHICH ONE MAN GOES FOR HOPE:

When Ron Quakkelaar was asked to fill in some interior cavities that had been left exposed after nearly a dozen skylights were roofed over at a Hope Network residential facility in Flint, Ron made the drive to check out the job, blueprints in hand and ready to hit the job running.

After arriving, he realized he'd need to pull a permit, and went to the City of Flint, where he was told that he'd first have to pass a test to be qualified to even perform work inside the city limits. Ron already possessed a state builder's license, but that wasn't enough. OK, said Ron, please give me the test.

Not so fast, he was told. You need to get fingerprinted first, to which he replied "You're kidding."

They weren't. So he went to a law enforcement agency, and they confirmed that indeed, they would fingerprint him.

But not today.

So Ron drove back to Flint a second time, got fingerprinted, and then went immediately back to City Hall. He was told he now qualified for the test.

But not today.

So Ron drove back to Flint a third time, took the test, passed, and finally performed the work.

If patience is a virtue, Ron Quakkelaar helped write the book on it.

DANNY *martinez*

LOOKING AT LIFE THROUGH THE WINDSHIELD, AND NOT THE REAR-VIEW MIRROR

I am sitting across from Dennis Martin, and looking into his eyes, can hardly believe what he is telling me, and yet, his advocate and mentor and counselor, Danny Martinez, nods to signify that it's likely true.

Dennis started off ordinary enough, or at least somewhat predictably. He sailed through grade school without much fanfare. "Good kid phase," he says. In middle school, he grew to be the class clown, but was getting good grades, and had his sights on becoming a doctor.

Then came high school, and Dennis began to court trouble.

His senior year, he quit school, and was kicked out of his dad's house. At 17, he came into some money from the sale of family stocks, and moved into an apartment above a bar in his hometown of Montrose.

At a Fourth of July party, he and less than a dozen others downed a keg of beer, three fifths of booze and smoked two ounces of weed. "I weighed 130," says Dennis, "but I drank most the keg myself."

He got into a fight that night and lost two teeth. The next day, he asked himself "What the hell happened?"

And went downhill from there.

Joseph Schreiber says of Danny: "I consider him a part of my family"

Dennis' story may not be typical, but it is somewhat representative of what Danny Martinez deals with as a substance abuse counselor employed by Hope Network and working at the Salvation Army Adult Rehab Center in Flint, MI.

His caseload includes upwards of 45 men, and he's been immersed in the program since 2003.

For many Hope consumers, Danny is a last resort and a last chance. They may have tried other programs and centers, and suddenly they're in Danny's care, Danny's circle, members of an intense, 180-day residential program. Some succeed; others don't.

"Danny is my main man," says Joe Schreiber, 22, a consumer convicted of one felony and five misdemeanors before enrolling in the program. "I've had a lot of counselors. But with Danny, well, I've told him some stuff I've never told anybody."

His face softens. "I'm talking trust."

Danny's office is in the basement of the Salvation Army. Some call it "The Cage." It measures 15-feet square. There are no windows, but plenty of stimuli, including some 500 Hot Wheels cars. (Six hundred more are stored at Danny's home). Model airplanes hover from the ceiling. It's a way to start conversations with men who fidget to reveal their pasts.

"I have lots of men with user parents, guys who never had a childhood," says Danny.

"So we play with the cars, with the planes; we revert to where they left off.

"With Danny, well, I've told him some stuff I've never told anybody."
—Joe Schreiber

"No more covering up."

The men with whom Danny works, he says, "have been kicked to the curb time and time again. They've been told they'll never be anybody, that they'll never amount to anything. So I put myself in their shoes. We try to break the cycle."

It's a fine line that Danny has to walk to serve as a professional, and also secure that trust. "I never address these guys as my clients. It's 'sir.' We have our boundaries, but we're friends, too. The kind of friend who cares, trusts. Someone you can talk to."

Which isn't to say he's soft. Danny demands that his charges live up to their daily contract. That means waking up on time, following rules, and putting in a full day's work on behalf of the Salvation Army loading trucks, picking up donations, manning the thrift store, and in the words of Danny, "making things happen for people in this community.

"They're giving back, and they're learning."

Some just barely make it. In Dennis' case, he recovered from the Fourth of July party just in time to spend the next untold number of days smoking and drinking himself nearly to death.

"I was smoking an ounce a day and doing a fifth a day," he recalls. "First thing in the morning, I'd 'wake & bake' with a doobie and just play video games. I could drink an 18-pack of Bud long-necks in one night."

His weight was down to 115 pounds, and by now, he was basically homeless, crashing at friends' homes, sometimes sleeping in his car. It was hunger that helped save him.

Dennis Martin: from homeless to Hope-ful with the help of Danny Martinez

"I was a mile and a half from my dad's house, and I was starving. 'Dad,' he said, 'I need some help.'"

Dennis' father eventually gave him a card with contact information for the Salvation Army in Flint, where Danny Martinez works.

Dennis fought the urge to check in, but finally relented, and in August of 2007 entered the program, successfully completing it in May of 2009. While a resident, he cleared up his obligations to the courts, earned his high school degree with a 3.3 GPA, quit smoking and got clean with alcohol and drugs. He enrolled at Mott Community College.

Looking back on the dangerous lifestyle to which he was addicted, he says today that "I'm surprised I lived through it."

He credits Danny in large part. "He's family to me," says Dennis.

As for Joseph Schreiber, he's got his sights set on a job so he can pay off some financial debts before enrolling in school himself. He's had at least eight jobs while living at the Salvation Army, using the experiences to build himself a resume.

He's also working hard to re-build his self-esteem, and looks to Danny Martinez for inspiration.

"I don't think I could ever do his job," Joseph says of Danny. "He never gives up on people. Not ever."

■ ■ ■ ■ ■ ■ ■

10 THINGS TO KNOW ABOUT DANNY MARTINEZ

1. He has no problem sharing his personal cell phone with consumers, even if it means being awakened at 3 in the morning to attend to a need.

2. When it comes time for consumers to pile into vehicles for a field trip, they'll do anything to ride shotgun in Danny's Jeep.

3. A native of San Antonio, Danny, 46, still has family there. A lifelong bachelor, he stays in close touch with his parents and sisters.

4. His past includes working at a state hospital in Missouri, and then as a forensic substance abuse counselor. He has vast experience dealing with high-risk abusers deemed not fit for the general community— pedophiles, serial killers, rapists.

5. His hobbies include deep-sea fishing, working on his computer skills, collecting Hot Wheels cars (he's got well over 1,000), and perfecting his artistry at barbecuing. He loves to sponsor cookouts for his Salvation Army family.

6. How he views his consumers? "There's not a thing I wouldn't do for any of these guys."

7. One of his favorite songs: "One Day at a Time" as sung by Joe Walsh.

8. Job he held right after graduating high school? "I worked as a translator in Costa Rica and Cancun."

9. He graduated in 1999 from Southwestern Assembly of God University in Waxachie, TX, with a degree in professional development.

10. Quote on the wall outside "The Cage" that serves as his office: "Look at life through the windshield, not the rear-view mirror."

Courtesy Photo

SWIMMING AND BIKING AND RUNNING FOR HOPE—ONE MAN'S QUEST TO PAY IT FORWARD

When Jon Turner dived into the waters of the Gulf of Mexico as part of an Ironman Triathlon he embarked on this past November, he was transported back to a far more sobering setting, if only for a moment.

That's when he was brought face to face during a meeting with wife Allison's team at Sojourners, Hope Network's inpatient neuro-rehabilitation program—and the important people who had a hand in bringing his wife back from a nearly fatal auto accident.

"I just broke into tears," he remembers. "I feel like I owe them the miracle of giving me my wife back. They're my heroes."

And in Jon's world, heroes should be recognized and rewarded for their efforts.

That's why he was willing to raise funds for Sojourners in conjunction with a monumental athletic endeavor that he attempted offshore of Panama City, Florida, when he subjected himself to the Ironman there, a grueling test of the human spirit that demands you consecutively swim 2.2 miles, bicycle 112 miles, then run a full-length marathon of 26.2 miles.

To prepare for his odyssey, Jon tested himself with half those distances—an accomplishment in itself—but far from the rigors of a full Ironman, a race that got its start in Hawaii and has blossomed in an international way to test an athlete's ability to swim, bike, run and transition among the three.

What makes Jon's quest especially significant is that he was in the same car in which his wife was injured—and suffered life-changing effects himself: a broken collarbone, shattered right elbow, fractured left ankle, concussion, and damaged cartilage and tendons.

Allison broke her left ankle, right wrist, pelvis, both orbital bones beneath the eyes and several ribs. She also sustained lung and liver damage, a fractured vertebrae in her neck, and a traumatic brain injury.

That accident, which occurred on February 21 of 2009, rendered both husband and wife into wheelchairs, and long stints of rehabilitation.

Today, though, they're both back to working full-time, and gaining on injuries that have only made them more resolved to leave the past in the past.

Jon and Allison, both 31, live in Grandville. He teaches residential construction classes to students enrolled at the Career Line Tech Center in Holland. She is an osteopathic physician completing her residency in a family practice.

Their lives were altered on that slippery February night when returning from Allison's parents' home in Greenville.

They were westbound and nearing Northland Drive NE when the car Allison was driving fishtailed, spun into the opposing lane, and was struck by another vehicle.

In the water, aboard a bike, and on the road... for 11 hours and 52 minutes.

They both lost consciousness at impact, and Jon remembers coming to and witnessing first responders tearing off the car's roof. The auto's engine had been catapulted off the chassis and 30 feet through the air. Through his haze, he recalls hearing the words "She's not going to make it to the hospital."

Jon had met the love of his life at Aquinas College, while he and Allison were both students. He'd graduated in 1998 from Holland West Ottawa High. She was a grad of Greenville High—Allison Turnbull at the time—same year. Both were involved in track, and it became their common bond. While both competed for Aquinas, he kidded her about how his workouts were tougher than hers. She gave it right back to him, twofold.

At Spectrum Health, Allison was put on a breathing machine and feeding tube. "She was way worse off than I was," says Jon, and even now, more than two years after the accident, you can sense the gravity in his tone.

In one respect, Jon healed more quickly than his wife, and was in on the decision where to send Allison after a month-long stay at Mary Free Bed Rehabilitation Hospital. In a quandary over options available to treat Allison for her brain injury, he asked one of her health care professionals what he would do if it were his wife or daughter.

"He didn't even blink," says Jon.

"Hope Network."

Jon and Allison at Mt. Ranier National Park, 2008

Specifically, that turned out to be Sojourners, where Allison spent three months with therapists and others.

Jon was so moved by the care his wife received there—and the very personal relationships both developed with staff—that he vowed to give back. He'd competed in road races and small triathlons before being injured, so settled on that as a way to raise money. But during his own recovery, he was warned that "You have to face the fact that you may never bike or run or swim again."

His reaction: "Screw that."

A year from that admonition, he told himself, "You're going to do a half-Ironman, and then a full Ironman."

During one of his first workouts after getting his legs back, he went to an area Y and tried for two miles on a treadmill.

"I barely made a mile," he says.

"Everything hurt. I was out of breath."

But the images of what Sojourners had done for Allison propelled him forward. Little by little, he gained on his workouts.

On Nov. 5 of this year, he attempted the full triathlon in Panama City.

What casual spectators witnessed was just another guy in a slick suit, stroking through the water and pedaling out to St. Andrews State Park and back, and then tramping a marathon.

What they didn't see were the half-dozen plates and 36 screws that help hold his body together.

What they may or may not have seen was that girl of his dreams, cheering him on, mind and body and soul.

And what they certainly didn't see was the impetus behind the act, the devoted people of Sojourners who helped deliver Allison back to her Jon.

Jon Turner not only accomplished his goal, but finished in 796th place out of more than 2,500 competing, with a stellar time of 11 hours, 52 minutes!

■ ■ ■ ■ ■ ■

Courtesy Photo

69

MAKING THEIR WAY
IN THE WORLD

LIFE ON THE FARM OFFERS SPECIAL REWARDS FOR HOPE CONSUMER

The first shards of morning are just rising in the east, and they find Liz White tramping in boots and a Carhartt jacket from the 163-year-old farmhouse she shares with her parents to the big barn looming yonder across the driveway.

She spends more than an hour cleaning stalls, feeding and watering the stock, and spreading fresh bedding for the critters. Each morning, she also leads the miniature horses out to start their day among the 15 acres tended by the family.

It's tough going some days because the body isn't always willing, and sometimes it's cold or snowing or raining. Farm work can be repetitive and monotonous, and it's not like the animals rise up to say thanks each day, or present you with a ribbon or a plaque or a pat on the back.

But Liz White presses on.

The farm helps give meaning and reason to her life. And Hope Network chips in as well, with an endeavor that puts not only pride into her pocket, but a little spending money and sense of purpose.

After her chores are completed, Liz trades in her shovel and pitchfork for more feminine trappings, immersing herself in a modest home business that is supported by Hope's Micro-Enterprise program.

The famous sugar scrub

Liz markets her scrub to anyone seeking to soften the skin on their hands and feet—and she has no trouble finding takers, in the cold dry months that define winter especially.

"It makes your hands and feet feel soft and smooth," says Liz, who sells her wares at craft shows, as well as one retail outlet near the stately family home, located midway between Grand Rapids and Coopersville on Four Mile Road NW just north of Interstate I-96.

**Grateful for Hope Network's input:
"They helped me learn how to
run a business."
—Liz White**

It's designed to provide business development services through one-on-one coaching and support to help men and women with developmental disabilities attain their highest potential.

For Liz, that means standing at the country kitchen counter and mixing up batches of "White's Sugar Scrub" that she produces from scratch.

"Oops, can't see that!" says Liz, as she hides the recipe from open view. Suffice to say that her concoction is made from sugar, grapeseed oil and glycerin.

Oh, and don't forget the essential aromatic scents. "A little on the top, and on the bottom," says Liz, putting a few drops of vanilla or orange or cinnamon or lilac into jars that will hold the product.

Liz folds the ingredients into a silver bowl, then spoons the mixture into two sizes of jars. After labeling each, they're ready for sale, at $4 for a four-ounce serving, and $8 for an eight-ounce container.

"It's a source of self-esteem," Liz's mother Mary says of her daughter's affiliation with Hope's Micro-Enterprise program.

"She loves it, and when she comes home from a craft show with money in her pocket, she's happy."

Trained in the art of marketing, Liz doesn't just show up and hope. Her little jars of comfort bear an attractive label, and, according to law, a list of ingredients. She'll lure you in with brochures and business cards.

Then there's the art of personally enticing passersby. "I talk to them," says Liz. "I tell 'em what it is, and how it's good for their skin. I open a jar and let them smell how nice it is."

Liz and her twin sister Emily, both 32, are the adopted daughters of Mary, 67, and husband Max, 69. The couple has one other adopted child in Rebecca, 24, as well as three biological children—Leigh Ann, 47, Brad, 45, and Todd, 41.

Working together as a family

The Whites spent their earlier years raising the family east of where they now are, and moved to the farm some 30 years ago, after Max and Mary spotted a For Sale sign in the front yard on a drive to Grand Haven.

Max was working as a controller for a major Grand Rapids area firm at the time, and had no idea his next life would be as a farmer. But the home spoke to them with the rhythms that agrarian life will beckon, and before they knew it, the Whites were raising goats, sheep and eventually, miniature horses.

While Liz made her way in special classes through Comstock Park and later Kenowa Hills school districts, she also made herself an integral part of the farm, as did all her siblings.

These days, she rises around 7 a.m. to care for the lone cat, six dogs, innumerable chickens and 16 horses.

The latter group receives the most, as they're bred and shown at fairs and exhibitions, and Liz and her family have countless ribbons and trophies for their efforts.

As the only child who still remains living at home, Liz also pitches in on several gardens on the grounds, although she's quick to admit "I don't like weeding." She says it, though, with a good-natured smile.

It's hard work all around, which provided a solid foundation to become part of Hope's Micro-Enterprise program, where attention to detail is paramount.

"She's a really hard worker, and really good at what she does," says Ron Irvine, program manager for the Micro-Enterprise effort, which works with more than a dozen consumers involved in their own businesses.

"Liz has overcome obstacles in her life, and has developed a drive that she gets from being passionate about her work. And she gets good results."

In Liz's spare time, she enjoys making scarves on a loom with her twin sister, taking in virtually all sports (especially basketball) and, of all things, doing laundry. "For some reason," says Mary, "she's a fanatic on laundry. She'd do it all day if she could."

Of making her sugar scrub, Liz says "It's a lot of fun," and of Hope Network's input, she's grateful: "They helped me learn how to run a business."

She is not one to complain, the product of parents who taught her to appreciate the value of hard work, and of working together. In fact, the only thing that gently irks here about the sugar scrub is one particular scent.

"The only scent I don't like," she says, and again while flashing her trademark smile, "is lavender."

Liz is one of six children who grew up on Mary and Max's farm

TOBY *janiga*

HOPE AGAINST ALL ODDS: TOBY JANIGA

The TV show "Survivor" has nothing on Toby Janiga.

By all rights, he was the sort of candidate to slip through the cracks. Another like him might have been swallowed up by the system. Lost in seas of red tape. Set adrift.

Instead, he bucked the odds, and today, Toby Janiga stands as living proof that even after enduring a revolving door of no less than 16 foster and group home placements, a person with challenges can create a life filled with hope and promise.

It didn't come easy. And there are no guarantees about the road ahead. But 10 minutes with Toby, and he'll convince you that life is worth the risks and the setbacks, and you can't help but cheer his corner.

His success story is so profound, that Toby, 32, was honored in 2010 at the annual Hope Network Legacy Gala, and presented the organization's "Independence Award."

"People told me I would never be able to own my own business, and that I would be in adult foster care my whole life," he says. "They told me I'd never live on my own, that I would never have a child.

"But I'm doing all the things they told me I'd never be able to do."

Toby's award is tied directly to his participation with Hope's Micro-Enterprise program, through which he initiated his own packing and shipping company in 2010, named Annabell's Express after his 5-year-old daughter.

But his story begins decades earlier, in Detroit, when at the age of 3, he became a ward of the state of Michigan because of his parents' substance abuse. That's when he started to bounce. He moved from a foster home to a children's hospital to a group home and ultimately, transported himself and his belongings a total of 16 times.

"Too many to count," he says of the number of elementary schools he attended.

As for middle schools, he attended three, then two high schools before moving onto a third—Sparta High—from which he graduated in 1998.

"All my life, all I heard was the negative."
—Toby Janiga

A lot of those formative years, he says, "were a blur," but he has especially vivid and painful memories of his pre-teen years, when he stayed in a group home.

"No one would listen to me. No one knew what I was going through. I used to think about who really wanted me, who really loved me."

Did he ever cry himself to sleep?

"Sometimes, yeah," he says.

He has all but lost touch with his biological parents, and he's no longer close with his only sibling, a sister.

But he made real gains during a nearly seven-year stay with his last set of foster parents, Albert "Bub" Hale and his wife Marilyn, who goes by "Mary." Toby credits them in large part for helping him establish his independence at the age of 17.

"I was working at Family Fare and I couldn't stand to wait for the bus anymore, he says. "I wanted a license, and my own car. I was falling in love, and I needed to move on. It was rough to start, but the Haleses helped me move on.

Courtesy Photos

Toby celebrated his graduation with the Hale family, Marilyn "Mary" (above) and Albert "Bub" Hale (below)

Christmas with the Hale family

Toby with Fred Idema

"I was out to prove to the world that I could succeed, that I didn't need to be in a group home, that I could hold a job, have a relationship."

Bub and Mary glow when they speak about Toby, who still stays in touch weekly. "He was our Valentine," remembers Mary, "because he came to us on Valentine's Day."

Bub and Mary, who live just outside Sparta, attended Friday's event, and can't say enough about Toby, just one of scores of foster children they've helped over the last 37 years. "We lost count at 60," says Mary.

Of Toby, Mary says "He had a real tough life. Some were good to him, but others were cruel," and the other foster placements were a mixed bag.

"We tried to show Toby a life of happiness," says Mary, who with her husband stressed to all their kids that "With the love of God, anything is possible."

They never doubted Toby would be successful. "He was always so willing to help," says Bub, "and he loves people.

"There was quite a lump in my throat" when Toby received his award, Bub noted.

After high school, Toby secured on-the-job training through a community based program, and left the Hales home at 23. Eventually, he got his own place at Stuyvesant Apartments near downtown Grand Rapids, where he now lives. He also earned a driver's license, and though his 1994 Dodge Intrepid will never turn heads, it's his.

He works part-time at a Big Lots store, stocking shelves at night. And for the last five years, he's worked with Hope's Micro-Enterprise program in multiple attempts to realize his entrepreneurial dreams.

His first foray into business was to design a litter box for cats that was disguised as a planter. His product, however, was too much like an existing one, and he decided to start anew.

His next effort focused on developing a jungle gym for cats, but the 12-foot-long prototype wouldn't fit in his car, so it was back to the drawing board.

"I have a million ideas," says Toby, and they continue to percolate. But in the meantime, he finds solace in Annabell's Express, which he instituted solely to support an Internet sales company that specializes in cabinet hardware.

It's called Keystone Accents, and its owner, Fred Idema, credits Toby with keeping things running smoothly, filling dozens of orders daily from around the world.

Though Toby technically has a developmental disability, he's able to process and ship material with hardly a glitch.

"He probably makes less mistakes than me," says Fred.

Toby smiles. "I've probably saved him a few times on shipping costs."

Fred knows something of Toby's history, and lauds him for his drive and persistence.

"I think he's overcome just an incredible amount of obstacles," says Fred, who sought help from Hope's Micro-Enterprises in an effort to help his business and give back to the community in what turned out to be a win-win combination.

Toby says the Independence Award he received last year helps to validate all the potential he felt inside, but had a tough time making others see.

"All my life, all I heard was the negative," he says.

"Now there's this award. And it's like I won't have to prove anything anymore."

JONATHAN *cermak*

Jonathan with his daughter Dannica

LEMONADE FROM LEMONS, AND HOW HOPE NETWORK HELPED SUPPLY THE SUGAR

Jonathan Cermak recognized one of the first responders to the scene of his accident, and he remembers imploring him to find an inhaler.

"I'm having an asthma attack," he managed to say.

The rescuer was stunned. "Kid, you're busted all to snot."

Which was true. It wasn't asthma, but a collapsed right lung. And that wasn't the worst of Jonathan's problems. He'd injured his brain in three separate places. The innermost layer of his carotid artery had collapsed. And he'd broken six ribs, a wrist, and most of the large bones south of his waist—his pelvis, the left femur, a tibia and fibula, and both ankles. For days, they pulled pieces of his shattered dashboard from his left knee.

The drunk driver who crossed four lanes of traffic to strike Jonathan head-on?

Treated and released for minor injuries. The courts gave him a year in jail—he served a total of 10 months—and five years' probation.

Jonathan, however, was left to lead a life of pain and suffering. But he counts Hope Network among the players who helped him come back from the brink of death.

Courtesy Photo

"Everybody there was just amazing."
—Jonathan Cermak on the staff
at Sojourners.

Jonathan spent his early years in Eaton Rapids, the son of a schoolteacher mom and a police officer. He grew up mostly in Portage, where his father Daniel serves as a patrolman today.

Jonathan, 29, comes from a long line of proud men and women who have spent their working lives in law enforcement—father, uncle, aunt and a cousin. And so it became his lifelong dream, one he was well within reach of when the accident changed the bearing on the compass he'd set so many years prior.

Even as a student at Parchment High School, he aspired to be an officer, earning a scholarship to Kalamazoo Valley Community

College from a law enforcement organization in that same county.

One of his first jobs as a young adult was as a security officer for a mall near his home. After that, he worked for the Kalamazoo Probation Enhancement Program, helping to coordinate efforts for inmates at a halfway house.

"I've just always had a huge interest in law enforcement," he says.

That dream came to a sickening halt, however, when he was 21, on the evening of Dec. 19, 2002. Jonathan was a freshman at Western Michigan University, and on his way home from work the first eve of winter break. Just a half-mile from home, his 1988 Oldsmobile was struck by a man at the wheel of a newer Chevy S-10 4X4 pickup.

Moments before, Jonathan had signed off with a co-worker with the words "Drive home safe."

Rescuers had to peel back the roof of his car to extricate Jonathan's broken body. He spent the next 12 days in a drug-induced coma, and at the outset, it was touch and go.

While his buddies enjoyed Christmas vacation, Jonathan stayed hospitalized well into January, then was transferred to a rehab facility in Vicksburg.

He couldn't walk. His speech was slurred. His left arm was useless, the result of the damage to his carotid, which in effect had caused a stroke that paralyzed his left side.

In the spring of 2003, he was moved from Kalamazoo County north to Hope Network's Sojourners facility in Grand Rapids, which provides transitional living services for people with brain or spinal cord injury. He would live there for four months, and it's where he learned in ways big and small how to battle back.

"I'm six-foot-five and weigh 215 pounds," he remembers of his stature upon entry into Sojourners some eight years ago, "and this little gal named Olivia, a physical therapist from Africa, I think, became my drill sergeant."

"She didn't put up with anything from me. I remember her pointing to a big mat table, and she said, 'OK, I want you to transfer up to the middle of the table, and then back again into your wheelchair.'"

The pain was excruciating. None of his joints would cooperate. The left arm sagged, and the bones in his lower body cried out in protest. It hurt everywhere.

"I was crying I was so frustrated," says Jonathan. "I slammed my shoes to the ground and screamed 'I hate this place.'"

But he didn't quit. Lemonade from lemons, he told himself.

Little by little—with prodding from Olivia and countless others—Jonathan Cermak walked, even though some wondered if he ever would again. He regained his speech, and he exited with only a cane for assistance.

"Everybody there was just amazing," he says of his stay at Sojourners. "I met some terrific people along the way."

Following his release from Sojourners, Jonathan underwent more than three years' intensive outpatient therapy back in Portage. He'd put college on hold for three years, but he returned, starting out with just a single class at WMU, and then adding more each semester.

He graduated in 2008 with a degree in Corrections, and along the way, found a wife in Nicole, whom he married in 2006. They have one daughter, Dannica, 5. They share a happy home on the outskirts of Kalamazoo with a dog and three cats.

Nicole is employed in food service. Jonathan—robbed of most the use of his left arm—might never be a police office. But he is making gains in law enforcement.

Today, he's a case manager in charge of delivering pre-trial services on behalf of the Calhoun County Sheriff Department in Battle Creek. His caseload numbers around 140. He also helps judges decide on a proper bond for those accused of a crime.

His dream is to one day become a probation officer, working closely with convicted criminals.

When he's not working, Jonathan pursues his other passion—the outdoors—especially when visiting property his grandparents own in northern Leelanau County.

"Outdoor is my passion," he says, adding that "My family and my hunting are the two things that mean everything to me. Hunting is really the only think that I have left, that wasn't taken away from me."

His comeback story, in fact, has been picked up by three outdoor publications, focusing on his tenacity in the face of injuries that might prompt another young man to sit it out.

But since the accident, he's resumed hunting everything from geese to turkey to deer. And even with one remaining bad arm, he's found ways to get the most out of life. That includes a sense of humor, remembering for instance, what it was like when little Dannica was just a tot, and wife Nicole was off to work.

"There I was, taking care of her alone at times," he says with a smile. "You ever try changing a 2-year-old's diaper with just one hand?!"

■ ■ ■ ■ ■ ■

Courtesy Photo

"LITTLE VICTORIES" FUEL PATRICK EWING'S REMARKABLE COMEBACK

For the better part of a month, he was stuck. Wouldn't clean the place. Wouldn't do laundry. Didn't cook for himself. Just kept falling deeper into depression.

"He told us he'd given up on himself, 100 percent," recalls Faith Doerzbacher, program manager of Hope Network Southeast's Enhanced Supported Independence Program (ESIP), near Mt. Clemens. "He was really going downhill, retreating a lot into himself."

That was the old Patrick Ewing, who had grown so accustomed to having his roommate Joseph perform daily affairs of living for the both of them that he felt incapacitated when Joseph moved out on his own.

"I panicked," says Patrick, 53, looking back on this past spring. "And I ended up in the hospital."

Today, though, Patrick is a new man. He takes care of his apartment, arranges transportation, shops for groceries, sticks to his schedule of medications, and looks forward to each new day as one brimming with fresh possibilities.

A native of the Detroit area, Patrick graduated high school in the mid-1970s, but as a freshman was injured in a motor vehicle accident. He was in a coma for 17 days, and initially couldn't move his right side. His recovery included physical and occupational therapy as well as speech therapy.

The Hope Network team (left to right): Residential Instructor Kathy Zatkoff, Program Manager Faith Doerzbacher, ESIP Coordinator Kenyatta Payton, with Patrick Ewing

"He did a 180... we're talking remarkable changes..."

He battled depression after high school, and even though he earned two associate degrees, couldn't land a job. He ended up at a semi-independent residential mental health care facility in the Mt. Clemens area, where he began to room with Joseph.

Looking back, Patrick now realizes that Joseph enabled him to avoid duties they should have been performing together. He laughs, in fact, to remember that at one point, he allowed others to draw

A man's home is his castle

him baths and clip his toenails—things he was capable of doing but didn't step forward to complete on his own.

It was just over five years ago that Patrick and Joseph moved into Brittany Park Apartments, where ESIP is headquartered. But in April 2011, Joseph had progressed to a point that he was ready to make a go of it on his own at the apartment complex, and eventually got his own place.

Faith and her staff noticed an immediate change in Patrick. "He was anxious, depressed," recalls Kenyatta Payton, an ESIP coordinator.

Things got so bad that Patrick ended up in a mental hospital and stayed most the month of August.

The turning point came when he was brought to a group home, and it was suggested he live there with 20 others.

Suddenly, all his options became clear, and with ongoing guidance from ESIP, Patrick realized he didn't need or want a group home setting.

"I said this ain't for me," Patrick recalls. "I like my space, and this was more care than I needed."

"He did a 180," says Kenyatta "We're talking remarkable changes, changes we never thought we'd see happen. Now, he does all his own cooking, laundry, cleaning—everything his roommate used to do."

It was slow going at first, when Patrick returned to Brittany Park. One challenge he faced was in setting his alarm clock after his unit lost electricity. The ESIP staff coached him through the process, and when the same thing happened a few weeks later, he called to say proudly that he'd re-set the timepiece without help.

"Those little victories are important," says Faith.

Laundry was another issue, "But we only had to show him one time," says Faith. "And as for shopping, we used to accompany him up and down the aisles, but he's got that down now, too."

Patrick is grateful to have a place of his own

Faith and her colleagues say it's exciting just to see the distinct changes in Patrick's mood and countenance: "No more gloom and doom," says Faith. "Now he's beaming, he's happy. He talks sports, cracks jokes. He's a completely other guy now, and it makes us so happy, makes us proud to be here for him."

Says Kenyatta: "His story makes us smile. Patrick has definitely captured our hearts."

Patrick blushes at all the accolades, but you won't catch him disagreeing. "I'm more energetic," he says. "I like myself better."

He smiles broadly at the mention of a visitor stopping by his apartment, which he was told ahead of time might happen.

"That's fine," he says. "I did the dishes, just in case."

■ ■ ■ ■ ■ ■

SHARON *wimmer*

MAKE A WISH; IT'S ON SHARON WIMMER!

Happy Birthday to you,
Happy Birthday to you,
Happy Birthday dear (insert any one of up to 700 names here),
Happy Birthday to you!

If you've worked during the last three years or so for New Passages, the latest and greatest addition to the Hope Network family, chances are you can't say your birthday has gone ignored.

You've got Sharon Wimmer to thank for it.

Not that she signed your card. Sharon, 64, is perfectly happy staying in the background, content to let you suspect that your birthday message originated from someone in the administrative ranks at New Passages.

But in truth, it's been Sharon lo these many months, working out of a modest office at the J-Town Clubhouse in Jackson, where virtually every weekday, she busies herself making sure your birthday is recognized with at least one letter directed to your mailbox.

"She's the best card-maker ever," says Jeff Sylvester, a member at the J-Town Clubhouse, where men and women with serious and persistent mental illness meet to embrace the world and one another.

Sharon is also a member at J-Town, where she takes her place alongside mentor Mary Moyer, a facilitator in the finance unit at the club, and turns out as many as 50 birthday cards per week, all sent compliments of New Passages.

They're not the sort of birthday cards you purchase at a store. Instead, each one is carefully rendered from card stock, then specially designed to coincide with a season or holiday that might fall around the same time as your birthdate. In a word—custom.

"I get the names and numbers from the corporate office," says Sharon, explaining how she knows the number of cards to complete per session. "For the month of October, for example, I have 35."

She pauses a moment to place a sticker on another card, then turns back to the conversation and smiles. "I gotta keep ahead of it."

Sharon's creations run the gamut. "You have to use what you have," she says. "Use your imagination and cut a lot of different things out of paper."

Mary is the perfect match for Sharon, since she's a long-time scrapbooker, and often lends the Clubhouse her own punches, ink stamps and other paraphernalia that go into making handcrafted cards.

"It's very rewarding," says Mary, as she gently supervises Sharon. "All these cards, and all done by hand."

The duo often relies on craft stores like Jo-Ann's or Michael's for supplies, although they're not above accepting donations and making do with snippets of paper and other whatnot they come across.

Materials that go into a card can include anything from sketches to three-dimensional objects to stickers to ribbons to glitter and more.

When Sharon has a batch of cards ready to mail, she hands them over to the corporate office, where they're placed into envelopes and

Mary Moyer and Sharon Wimmer share a smile

Sharon's not in it for the money, but to help make a difference.

89

mailed to New Passages employees about to celebrate another year of living.

Sharon's own life began in Trenton, N.J., but she moved at an early age to Jackson and graduated from Western High School in 1965. She worked in an S&H Green Stamps store for awhile, then for a factory that manufactured surgical garments.

She and husband John make their home in Jackson, sharing space with a gray cat named "Smoky Link" that sports black rings around its tail.

They don't have much family in the Jackson area, so Sharon is always eager to spend time at the Clubhouse. She's grateful for the day she was chosen to assist Mary as card-maker extraordinaire. "I was lucky to be picked, and it's a real learning experience."

In her spare time, Sharon devotes time and energy to conservation projects. "I like nature, especially keeping the oceans clean, and I'm interested in the preservation of our parks, our natural resources."

Sharon is paid 50 cents for each card she completes, and can turn out a dozen or so a day, but her expenses largely come out of her pay, so nobody's getting rich.

But it's obvious she's not in it for the money. Instead, Sharon feels enriched by the opportunity to make a little difference in all the lives of those who count themselves part of the Hope Network New Passages family, even if it's for a scant moment one day of the year.

"She's a very hard worker who always tries to do her best," Mary says of Sharon. "She does a great job and she's very dependable.

Mary works in the finance department, and she also serves as a mentor to Sharon

"She's here for me."

And in truth, she's also "here" for a lot more of us—sitting in a little office on a busy street in Jackson, crafting birthday cards for hundreds of people annually, most of whom she'll likely never meet.

■ ■ ■ ■ ■ ■

IT'S ALL IN THE CARDS

Editor's Note: Here at CAKE headquarters, we got to thinking it might be nice to reciprocate Sharon Wimmer for all the warmth she sends others' way. So we're going to share two little elements, and leave the rest up to you!

One, Sharon Wimmer's birthday is December 15th.

And two, here's her work address: Sharon Wimmer, c/o J-Town Clubhouse; 1200 N. West Avenue; Jackson, MI 49201

DEREK O'NEAL: HOPE NETWORK'S OWN MUSIC MAN!

One minute, he was the high-flying vice president of a major financial firm, boasting a past that included graduation from an Ivy League college and an illustrious career with the military.

In the next, he was transformed by the deer that struck his vehicle into a netherworld where brain-injured victims walk a tight-rope between darkness and light, then and now, life and death.

Nobody knew how he might emerge.

But thanks to an indefatigable attitude, and a roadmap charted in part by a team from Hope Network in East Lansing, Derek O'Neal is not only back among the living, but an effervescent poster child for All Things Possible.

Then, too, there is the music.

Derek collects it, records it, plays it and sings it. In fact, it was commonplace to hear him belting out all kinds of songs during the months he roamed the hallways at Hope's Lansing Rehabilitation Services, a complex of buildings tucked away in a wooded setting just minutes from the Michigan State University campus.

"We should have you come back once a month to serenade the halls," quips Jeff Frommeyer, a social worker at the East Lansing Hope complex. But Frommeyer is serious when he emphasizes how

"inspirational" Derek's been for staff and other consumers served by Hope.

"I've been here nearly eight years, and his is the story that I remember most. There is a handful that stands out, but he had to recover so much of his cognitive skills. He had to come back completely, and he has. He's basically re-routed his life. And he's done it with determination and a positive attitude."

Derek says "Thank you" softly, and it's not too long before he's singing, punctuating the conversation with a half-dozen launches, singing everything from jazz to pop to his all-time favorite, Johnny Mathis.

His voice runs through a few bars of "Don't Worry, Be Happy" as sung by Bobby McFarren, and as he comes to a close, laughs easily and says, "I feel the Lord gave me a second chance, and choices. Why NOT be happy? Why NOT look forward to the next day. Things are gonna be alright!"

Derek with Program Assistant Shauna Nance

You might, however, not blame Derek for feeling otherwise, considering what happened the night of June 7, 2004, when a deer ran onto the highway and crashed through his windshield.

Derek was traveling 70 miles per hour on Highway 696, some 85 miles from the home in Okemos he shares with wife Rene and their son Jadon, 9. (The couple has four other children with previous spouses, ages 19 to 24.) He was lucky to even survive the collision.

His critical care included treatment at no less than three hospitals over the next few months, surviving a trio of delicate surgeries to address a serious brain injury that left him in a coma for two months.

At one point, Derek was disoriented to such a degree that he

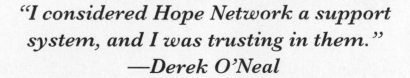

"I considered Hope Network a support system, and I was trusting in them."
—Derek O'Neal

tried to escape from a Hope Network office under the notion that he was being held as a Prisoner of War. Though he's progressed far beyond such illusions, he still receives treatment through the Hope facility in East Lansing, with a special emphasis on addressing his short-term memory loss.

Derek never imagined while growing up in New York among privileges reserved for the very few, that he would have serious health issues as a relatively young man.

The eldest of nine children, Derek graduated from New York City's prestigious Stuyvesant High School, then earned degrees at William & Mary, as well as Embry-Riddle Aeronautical University.

He spent 15 years in the U.S. Army, including service during Operation Desert Storm in Iraq and Kuwait. He retired as a major, and afterward secured work as a vice president for an automotive supplier. Derek left that position to accept a job as an executive with a financial holding group, a post he held just six months. That's when the catastrophic accident occurred.

Derek with his wife Rene and son Jadon

The crash plunged his life into an abyss that science still struggles to understand. Friends and family were no longer instantly recognizable. His speech suffered.

Some physical activities were no longer easy to perform. And memories wouldn't surface.

"Today," says Derek, "I'm a husband and a dad and I'm still Derek. "I'm just a different Derek."

In a unique way to establish order, define his road back, and share with others, Derek put together a compact disc entitled "Magic of Music" that should perhaps should be required viewing for anyone who has had to face adversity.

He's shown the program to countless groups—anything from service organizations to other folks battling brain injury. The CD tracks the story of his life, the accident, and then how he used music to help gain footholds on a future.

"Music," he says, "is an integral part of our culture" and Derek points out that it can help us to create awareness, to heal and to love.

"I sang everywhere I went," says Derek, "although I confess that my son Jadon, when I would be singing in a mall, would tell me 'Not cool, dad.'"

He also leaned heavily on medical teams affiliated with the hospitals, and with staff at Hope Network in East Lansing. "I believed in what Hope was doing for me," he says. "I considered Hope Network a support system, and I was trusting in them."

Today, Derek is enrolled at Lansing Community College in pursuit of a job as a paralegal—no small task considering the struggle he continues to endure in regaining his cognitive skills.

"Paralegal is taught in a different language," says Rose Roberts, a speech-language pathologist at Hope in East Lansing. "But Derek pursues it doggedly, and keeps such a positive mental attitude. He's very inspirational to all of us."

Brooke VanBuren-Hay, Ph.D., is a psychology services supervisor at the East Lansing center, and says that Derek "had to incorporate a lot of changes into his life.

"Though he had to deal with a lot of 'nos' and 'not yets,' he would come back the next day and say, 'What do I have to do?'

"He's resilient."

Sadly, one of Hope's staff who pitched in wholeheartedly to help Derek—registered nurse Christine Schneider—died in December 2009. But Derek will always credit her with helping him face some of his toughest times.

"Christine was a big part of it," says Derek. "She believed in me, and she represented everyone else at Hope Network who felt the same.

"They put me back together."

■ ■ ■ ■ ■ ■

Brooke VanBuren-Hay, Ph.D., Derek and Shauna Nance—what a team!

MOVED BY THE SPIRIT

PASTOR JOAN CORNELISON—HELPING US ALL TO REMEMBER "THAT THEY ARE WHOLE"

With a deep breath, Pastor Joan Cornelison summons the courage it takes to reveal a slice from her past that is not common knowledge among her Hope Network family. Combined with other events in her life that led to a change in both attitude and direction, she refers to it as "The Stripping."

"When you walk with the Lord," she says, "you have to expect storms."

The year was 1989, and she was a young woman of 26 living a privileged life in Kenya, on the verge of everything she thought held hope and promise for her future.

"The wedding dress was ready," she says sadly. "We were three months away."

And then, in a tragic accident that would forever change her life, those close to her fiancé Joseph, and the couple they would have become, her groom-to-be drowned.

An evangelist, Joseph had been preaching during an all-night session in Nairobi, and to celebrate, went for a swim in the hotel pool where he was lodged. A cramp overcame him in deep water, and efforts to save him failed. Pastor Joan was informed by a phone call, and drove eight hours to hold him one last time, to say her goodbyes.

"It threw me into a void," she remembers. "I was desperate. And I couldn't handle the grieving" among her church family, which numbered an astronomical 10,000 members.

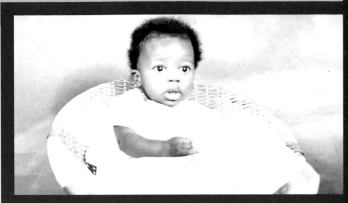

Photos from her childhood in Eldoret, Kenya

Before emigrating to the United States in 1996, Pastor Joan had been raised in Kenya, the daughter of parents who both commanded high diplomatic positions—her father in Uganda, and her mother in the family's homeland.

She spent her youth and adolescence without want, and attended the best schools. By her mid-20s, she was en route to earning a doctorate, but by this time more to please her status-minded family than for her own satisfaction.

Three months after losing her betrothed, her home was robbed while she sang choir in a church service. The thieves took everything—right down to the pillowcases, teaspoons, even the memories inherent in photos and scrapbooks and mementos.

"Thus began my personal struggle," she says of that period some 21 years ago. She fell victim to stress, became sick, finding her way back in part through sweet solace in the words of a pastor who advised her that "Life will not be easy, but the hand of the Lord will never leave you."

Today, Pastor Joan (pronounced as two syllables: Jo-ANN) leans on those words every day in her capacity as Hope Network's Director of Pastoral Services. She directs a three-person crew whose job it is to link Hope consumers to faith groups of their choice.

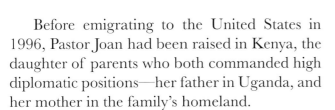

> ### Pastor Joan is moved by the Lord to pray, to lift others up, to dance!

They do it through myriad activities, but also with no small amount of listening, choosing to patiently spend time with people as opposed to the proselytizing that can often define persons of the cloth.

It has taken her most of a lifetime to realize it, but Pastor Joan—despite all her formal education and practicums—knows she can't always solve everyone's problems. Instead, "I simply walk with them.

"I let God be God. No formulas."

That may not be the panacea some seek for their spiritual life. And it's not that Pastor Joan won't remedy something she can, or that she doesn't believe in miracles. She does.

It's just that she finds it equally important—and especially so with Hope's diverse community—to "celebrate who they are, as they are, knowing that God is present in their lives and mine."

"That they are whole."

Her mission is especially evident in the building where she works on Hope Network's 36th Street Campus, which hosts dozens of men and women with physical and cognitive challenges. Consumers spend weekdays there until 2:30 p.m. involved in activities designed to enrich their lives.

Watching Pastor Joan make the rounds into rooms designed as "teams" is to see joy in the faces of those who recognize her and call out her name.

"Hey Pastor! Hi Pastor!" says a man clutching "The Silly Kid Joke Book." He shakes her hands and then says something unclear, except for the word "heaven."

She moves on within the same room. "Good to see you," she exclaims to a young woman. "You still going to friendship group at your church?" A hearty nod and smile tell her yes.

Someone presses a leaflet into her hands. It's an invitation to attend the consumer's church service.

As she's leaving, a young man with an intent look on his face approaches and asks Pastor Joan the question he's been posing every time he's seen her for the last eight years: "Is the devil a liar?" He then struggles to convey that he might not qualify for an outing that day.

She engages him in a conversation that shows she cares, and it ends with her telling him firmly that he has to obey rules, and that even if he doesn't get to go today, "God does give second chances."

Pastor Joan was born and raised in Bungoma, in western Kenya, and was expected by her parents to pursue academic greatness. She complied, using a flashlight under her bedcovers to quench an insatiable appetite for reading—everything from Nigerian novelist Chinua Achebe to Dickens to Dostoyevsky.

After attending private schools and graduating a university, she was one of just two out of 800 to qualify for a master of arts and literature program. Though gifted and apparently soaring, she felt disconnected while isolated in academia's ivory tower.

The "Personal Stripping," as she described, helped her realize that "Everything in life is movable—your job, friends, finances, reputation.

"The only thing that's immovable is the Lord Jesus Christ, and so that's where I grip with both hands, when there is nothing else. And God always comes through. Maybe not right away. But eventually, He does."

Pastor Joan had to rely on that faith when both parents died (her father in 1999 and her mother in 2006) and again more recently, when her older brother died in a traffic accident in Kenya just months ago. In 2008, Pastor Joan's brother-in-law died from an asthma attack, and just months later, the same sister lost a daughter at age 12, from complications involving brain damage following a bicycling accident five years earlier.

She buoys herself with her work, which, boiled down to three words, is this: "I serve people."

Her days begin at 5:30 a.m. with quiet time, during which she prays bedside on her knees. She closes her evenings with thanks. Often, she's joined in prayer by her children—son Jonathan, 3, and daughters Micaela, 10, and Kelis, 8.

Pastor Joan holds several degrees and certificates, but perhaps none is as important as the clinical pastor education she received in 1997 at Bronson Hospital in Kalamazoo. It helped her abandon whatever "Messiah complex" she might have been flirting with, and realize she simply needed to embrace people in need.

She eventually earned a Masters of Divinity degree, and joined Hope Network in 2002, first as chaplain, and in 2006 as director of pastoral services.

Pastor David Veldt, who until recently served as Hope's Minister for Consumer Services, calls Pastor Joan "our pilot," noting that

"She plays a cool role because she's in the organization's leadership, yet still gets to interact with the consumer."

Margie Brenner, the department's administrative assistant for several years, says "Pastor Joan is definitely a visionary," adding, "She sees the big picture, and helps us to see it beyond what we do day-to-day."

Pastor Joan—whose role as a single mom via a divorce she accepts as part of life's humbling journey—believes strongly

that "God has a purpose for every human being," but the difficult part is taking the time to see it surface in everyday people.

"We're too preoccupied—making deadlines, going to meetings. But if we wait long enough—if you're patient—you will experience the gifts that everyone brings to this life.

"If you treat people with dignity," she says, "you will see so much beauty coming out of them."

AND WHEN SHE'S NOT PASTORING...

1. By her own admission, Pastor Joan is "a phenomenal Irish dancer," a throwback to her days at St. Brigids school in Kitale, Kenya, where the headmistress hailed from the Isle of Erin itself. "They used to look for the lean and tall," says Pastor Joan, who stands 5'8". Somewhere, she says, there's a picture of her in an emerald green outfit with a yellow sash. Will she dance at the office Christmas party? Probably not. But in the privacy of her Grand Rapids home, she'll bounce a bit for her kids.

2. She loves to read. Belongs to a book club through the Grand Rapids YWCA. Loves the selection by Kathryn Stockett, entitled "The Help."

3. Loves to cook, too. "Ninety-nine percent of my meals are still Kenyan." Think spicy, aromatic sauces; garlic and cloves and peppers. "It keeps me in touch with my roots."

4. Pastor Joan helps conduct services twice monthly at a retirement community church, but attends Grand Rapids First in Wyoming, where she preaches not. "I just inhale," she says.

5. Pastor Joan may be one of a very few who was awarded a full scholarship to Calvin Theological Seminary—and turned it down. She instead chose United Theological Seminary in Dayton, Ohio, where she paid her own way and earned her Master of Divinity degree.

6. How she keeps herself humble? She was conducting a workshop with some men and women of Team D, and when she asked for a definition of faith, a man who had been completely silent the entire time raised his hand. "Faith," he answered, "is walking up that aisle and saying you will live with this person until you die."

"I laughed," says Pastor Joan. "So profound. You take that, Pastor Joan. And you went to the seminary!"

101

ALZHEIMER'S CAN'T STOP THIS LOVABLE LITTLE DYNAMO FROM SPREADING HER SPECIAL BRAND OF GRACE

Because she suffers from Alzheimer's, Silvestra Del Valle can't convey much about the 101 years she's lived and learned on this earth.

But in her own indomitable way, she serves as a sparkplug and poster child for a Hope Network isle of comfort where seniors can spend the day surrounded by people who know that there is dignity even when our minds and voices have been compromised.

It's called "Side By Side," a haven within the brick walls of Family Life Center, what used to be a convent for Carmelite nuns on the west side of Grand Rapids. It's where Silvestra counts herself among some 20 men and women who visit almost every weekday, immersing themselves in everything from friends to food to flora.

"Ah, rosa, rosa, hermosa rosa," says Silvestra, caressing the petals of the "beautiful rose" gracing "The Living Garden" which is the outdoor centerpiece of this Hope respite center.

And then, she's turning the corner to feast her eyes on a statue of the Blessed Virgin Mary. "Mary and all the saints," she says through a translator. "They're all my saints," and with a reverence honed from years of worship, she makes three signs of the cross and leans forward on her spindly legs to kiss the Virgin's cheek.

"Ya, ya, ya," she says softly.

It is a scene repeated daily here, at 1256 Walker Avenue NW, where Silvestra arrives each morning before 9 to commune with others who take advantage of enrichment activities designed to improve social, educational, psychological and physical challenges of its participants.

Her favorite venue are the gardens, where water features compete with lush stands of annuals and perennials, as well as vegetables specifically planted to remind clients of gardens they tend or once tended in earlier lives.

When she's not walking among the plant life, Silvestra is inside, busy teasing both staff and others served by the program.

"I think Silvestra thinks of me as her grandson," says Side by Side staff member Tom Bulgarella. "She's determined to keep me in line. And even though there's a language barrier, I can pick up on some of her words, and I know when she's scolding me." He grins. "She's quite a character, and truly incredible."

Silvestra was born in 1910 in the town of San Lorenzo on the Caribbean island of Puerto Rico. Her parents labored to harvest and manufacture tobacco and other crops that surround the city of 37,000, and it was at an early age Silvestra grew to know hard work as well.

At 41, she moved to the United States, settling in Philadelphia with husband Jose. She followed daughter Carmen Rivera to the Grand Rapids area, establishing a home here in 1977.

Silvestra's husband died three years ago, prompting Silvestra to move in with Carmen and her husband, who would die just one and

Silvestra with (left to right): Sandra Sala-Jasinki, Program Manager for Side by Side, and Teresea Schlump, Director of Elderly Programs at the Family Life Center

a half years later. Now it's just the two of them, and Carmen and her mother share virtually everything, right down to the queen-sized bed in the modest home they keep in Wyoming.

"She can't sleep alone," says Carmen, 58, who is employed in housekeeping at a local hotel and spends spare time doting on her mother.

Suddenly, a red Hope Network bus pulls alongside the curb. It's Silvestra, coming home after a full Wednesday of activities at Side by Side. She steps through the door, greets Carmen and her

"Everybody loves her... how can you not?"

friend Evelyn, shakes a visitor's hand, then announces she's tired: "Estoy cansado!"

It's 3:45 in the afternoon when Carmen helps her mother into bed, fetches her a glass of water, and then waits for the inevitable: Silvestra will rest but 10 minutes before she's off and running again.

"Before you know it, she's outside," says Carmen, who sometimes with Evelyn's help, will monitor Silvestra as she bounces up and down their street to visit with neighbors, smell the flowers in their front yards.

At Side By Side, Silvestra will spend quiet times with friends she's made like Juanita, who is hard of hearing. But in her active moments, Silvestra enjoys using her voice to rhyme words, and to mimic in timbre and tone the voices of others that she hears during the day.

"She likes to tease a little bit, and she likes the rhyming words," says Teresea Schlump, director of elderly programs at the Family Life Center.

The Center threw a 100th birthday for Silvestra in 2010, and as she approaches her 102nd, she shows little signs of slowing.

Though she has but two teeth, they are her own. She takes only one medication on a daily basis. And she is picky about what she eats, preferring rice and fish and beans to standard American fare.

Silvestra never imbibed or used tobacco, though she does confess to a few "vices" like hard candy and orange soda.

The highlight of most her days is going to Side By Side, says Carmen. Though she sometimes thinks she's visiting someone or

Courtesy Photos

Silvestra with her husband Jose and children Leoni, Cookie, Carmenduz and Ada in San Lorenzo, Puerto Rico (1940) Tito not pictured

Silvestra with Tito (1940)

something in her old hometown of Philly, Carmen lauds the Hope Network staff for being "wonderful with my mother's care.

"My mother is a full hand, and yet they are really patient with her."

Teresea Schlump likes to think everyone enrolled at Side By Side is the recipient of special attention, whether they're taking a nap, enjoying a jigsaw puzzle, visiting with others or involved in a special activity.

At 100 years old and holding, though, it's difficult to miss the effect and hold that Silvestra has on the others.

"I know everybody loves her from the start," says Teresea. "How can you not?"

▪ ▪ ▪ ▪ ▪ ▪

WHAT MAKES SILVESTRA UNIQUE:

1. She only got as far as the third grade, but is smart enough to know that Americans eat too much bread. "It makes them soft," she says.

2. Silvestra's got a sweet tooth, especially for butterscotch candies, M&Ms and lollipops.

3. For reasons unknown, she likes to keep paper towels wadded up in her pockets. "Ma, you're pregnant with paper," daughter Carmen will tell her.

4. In all her 100 years, Silvestra has never learned to drive a motor vehicle.

5. Her favorite reading material? The West Michigan Hispanic newspaper "La Voz."

6. Her height? Four feet, 5 inches. And her weight? Just 78 pounds.

7. In her day, Silvestra was an accomplished seamstress. She used to sew her own clothes, and created others for sale.

8. Speaking of clothes, Silvestra wears skirts and dresses, period. "Pants," she says, "are for men."

S ince my youth, O God, you have taught me, and to this day I declare your marvelous deeds. Even when I am old and gray, do not forsake me, O God, till I declare your power to the next generation, your might to all who are to come.

—Psalm 71: 17-18

Consumer Bob Kuiper strums along on his guitar

A HEAVENLY MATCH IN CALVARY CHURCH AND HOPE'S WILDWOOD VILLAGE

Where two or three are gathered unto my name, I am in the midst of them."
—*Matthew 18:20*

Some of the speech is slurred.

Some of the notes errant.

The bodies still struggling to heal.

But as the psalmist wrote, they "make unto the Lord a joyful noise," and who could argue that Jesus himself isn't sitting among them, accepting their gracious gifts from hearts and heads that may have been injured, but won't be stilled.

Even against the backdrop of injuries and trauma that have affected their brains and limbs, more than a dozen residents from Hope Network's Wildwood Village gather every other Tuesday to give thanks and praise.

For an hour, they sing and celebrate God's word, part of a larger effort by Hope Network's Pastoral Services to pair its many residences with churches. It's a visceral way of providing a ministry to Hope consumers who have had to battle back against the debilitating effects of strokes, auto accidents and other life-changing events that might rob them of the ability to fully walk, talk or function in conventional social circles.

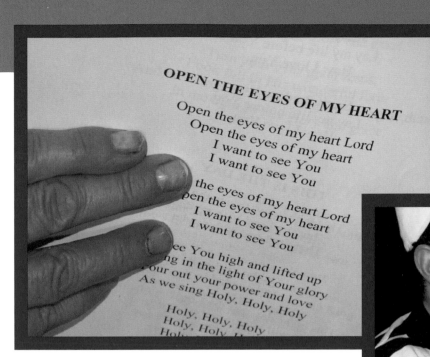

OPEN THE EYES OF MY HEART

Open the eyes of my heart Lord
Open the eyes of my heart
I want to see You
I want to see You

the eyes of my heart Lord
pen the eyes of my heart
I want to see You
I want to see You

ee You high and lifted up
ng in the light of Your glory
our out your power and love
As we sing Holy, Holy, Holy

Holy, Holy, Holy
Holy, Holy,
Hol

Sharing in the good news

"This partnership has given the consumers at Wildwood meaning and the will to go on," says the Rev. Joan Cornelison, Hope Network's director of pastoral services. "They know that no matter how difficult the journey, they are not alone."

Indeed. On any Tuesday night they convene, their sense of community and spirit is palpable. "The Lord doesn't mind how we sound," Kathy Higbee says from the wheelchair that's been a constant companion since a car accident some 20 years ago.

And in the next moment, the group is breaking into the soft strains of "How Great Thou Art," the guitar music provided this evening by resident Bob Kuiper, who's sitting in for regular accompanist Mario Duron.

Normally, Mario teams with Chuck Ely and Jackie VanderPoel, both of whom are here this night. The trio hails from Calvary Church in Grand Rapids, where members of the special-needs ministry agreed five years ago to team with Hope Network at Wildwood, a residential campus specializing in the care of brain-injured adults,

"It's an honor to watch each and every one of them grow in their faith."
— Sue Allen

and located just a few miles down the road on East Beltline Avenue.

"The things these people have lived through helps me to realize that the small things that happen to me are insignificant," says Chuck, who owns a marketing company. "These people are very inspiring to me."

Adds Jackie: "This is not a burden for us whatsoever; we love being here."

And yet, the people to whom the Calvary group is ministering only return the favor in lauding what the three are doing for them.

Kathy Higbee says, "The Lord doesn't mind how we sound"

"I'd like to say thank you to Chuck and his team for giving up their time and bringing such joy to the people sitting here," says Mike Clifford, still dealing with the effects of an auto accident 30 years ago.

Behind Mike, the sun is setting on a snowy scene just outside Wildwood's picture window, almost belying the pain and suffering some of these residents have gone through in their recovery process.

But ever the optimist, Mike notes that "It's extraordinary what the Lord enables us to remember," and in the next moment, Bob strums a G-chord on the guitar, and the group of faithful is into its second hymn, "My Hope Is Built on Nothing Less."

"It's an honor to watch each and every one of them grow in their faith," observes Sue Allen, a recreation assistant at Wildwood. "And some of them obviously have tough questions."

Following a half hour of song, the group looks to Chuck to lead a discussion. Tonight, it focuses on "Water is Life," with plenty of examples from the Bible. Kathy reads from hers, and though the words don't come easy from her lips, the message is clear: Christ is the living water.

Chuck Ely leads the group in prayer

"Without water, there is not life," says Chuck, and heads nod in agreement, their voices extolling both the literal and figurative meanings of water—the kind that slakes our thirst, and the sort our souls need for spiritual nourishment.

"Some people might try to satisfy their thirst with cars, drugs, alcohol," says Chuck, "when it's the word of the Lord we should be searching for."

After closing with The Lord's Prayer, the group mingles, and some volunteer their pasts.

Don Livingston suffered through a car accident 20 years ago.

Lori Wissink was on a date on Valentine's Day 31 years ago when the car in which she was riding was struck by a train.

One resident speaks of an accident during the late 1960s, and in the next breath is regaling how he once played baseball with the Detroit Tigers and drove in the Indianapolis 500, not memories, but leftover effects of his injury.

No one here is judged, however—only comforted—and especially on Tuesdays when they support one another in music, verse and prayer.

They've also traveled together. When possible, some of Wildwood's residents attend regular church services at Calvary. They've also taken in a couple of concerts. And their tender story was featured in the Religion section of The Grand Rapids Press in its Easter 2008 edition.

"Here we are, just a little Bible study, but just think of the stuff we've done in five years," says Chuck, to the obvious delight of the group.

"You bring us the Word of the Lord," says Bobby Williams. "And God understands."

■ ■ ■ ■ ■ ■

Hearts and hands join in prayerful song to the Lord

LEAVING A LEGACY

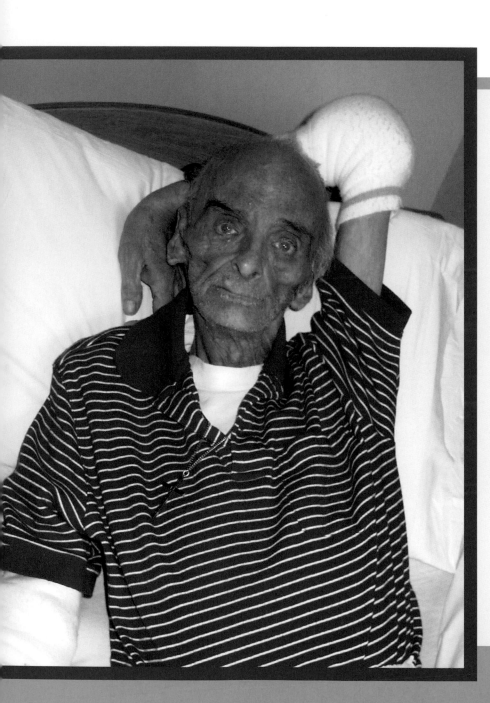

EDSEL *mcdonald*

SMALL SPACES AND GENTLE GRACES: THE LIFE OF EDSEL MCDONALD

Some 30 hours after interviewing Edsel McDonald for The Book of CAKE, the 70-year-old cancer patient died quietly in his room at a Jackson health facility. Among his last words to writer Tom Rademacher: "Thanks for telling my story."

Edsel McDonald never learned how to read or write well. He barely finished the second grade. At no time did he ever own a car, and never learned to drive. He grew up poor and lived in squalor, staying for a period in a house condemned. At least once, he was beat up by intruders who stole his meds.

He was born and lived and died in the town of Jackson, Michigan, and claims that in all his 70 years, never traveled even far enough to gaze at a Great Lake. He battled schizophrenia and spent some time behind bars. He earned what he could by teaming with his brother Robert. Together, they delivered the Jackson Citizen-Patriot in a little wagon they pulled behind them.

Before Edsel was diagnosed with lung cancer, he smoked three packs of Raleighs a day.

For someone whose world was so very limited—for someone who never grew to be wealthy or powerful or a font of influence—this long-time Hope Network consumer taught us in his final moments what it is to live with quiet grace and humility.

Courtesy Photo

Edsel (left) with his brother Robert

"He's taught me patience, understanding and compassion."
—Rose Mary Titler, R.N.

Edsel with Alesha Prelesnik, his case manager with Hope Network Southeast in Jackson

He was born to Charles and Mary in June 1940. His early years were grim. Without being specific, he says his childhood included beatings. A rough life? "Yes, most of the time," and says he and his brother endured by following this precept: "Just stay out of trouble, behave, and do what you're told."

On one occasion when Edsel visited his parents' gravesite, social worker Debbie Cooper overheard him whisper "You guys be good, and don't fight."

For most his life, he was "in the system," fighting his mental illness and taking advantage best he could of services offered by Jackson County. In later life, some described him as cantankerous and demanding. But beneath his raw surface, they also glimpsed a

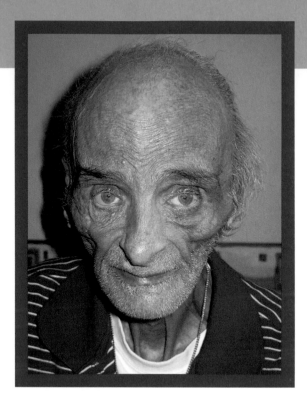

man who'd suffered and had to fight hard just to survive. Virtually everywhere he went, he walked.

His final residence—Jackson County Medical Care Facility—were probably the best digs he'd ever enjoyed, said Alesha Prelesnik, a case manager with Hope Network Southeast in Jackson.

He moved there after learning he had fourth-stage lung cancer, celebrating a room with a radio and TV and clean sheets. He was sitting in a wheelchair just outside the door when I walked in to meet him.

"I do pray" was one of the first things Edsel told me, and that he enjoyed listening to Family Life Radio, which broadcasts nationwide. When I asked him what he prayed over, he answered "That's between me and God," then smiled thinly and added "Maybe I'll tell you next time you visit."

While I was fairly certain there wouldn't be a next time, Edsel's advocates agreed that he possibly never understood the severity of his diagnosis, partly because of his schizophrenia.

"He gets it to some extent," said Debbie Cooper, who has worked closely with Edsel for nearly a year, "but he doesn't really believe it.'

Since his admittance into the county-run facility, Edsel aston-ished workers there. "He's quite resilient," said Edsel's physician, Heather Simpkins, M.D. "We expected him to die months ago. We've all grown to love him here, and we'll be sad to see him go."

In fact, more than one person had walked in on Edsel during the last few weeks and thought he had died. At one point, his respi-ration was down to a scant four breaths per minute. Twice in recent

weeks, a priest was summoned to admin-ister last rites.

"He's had every single symptom of death," said his case manager Alesha. "I'd sat in his room several times where I was just waiting to call staff. I kept waiting for his chest to rise."

But Edsel fooled them all, and in the next moment would be summoning enough lunch to feed three people. On his last full day on earth, he wheeled himself up to aide Starlet Dentmond's desk and asked her to call into the kitchen an order of five eggs over easy, two sausages, a bowl of corn flakes, coffee and juice.

"And he'll eat every bit of it," she said with a laugh.

Starlet, too, had been surprised at Edsel's ability to rebound. "It's amazing to me how long he's been here. There were days when we were sure we were going to come back to work the next day, and he'd be gone."

Irony gently surfaced soon after Edsel arrived at the care center. Though terminally ill, he decided he was there for the long haul, and asked Nichole Babineau, LPN, to write down the names of all those who touched his life there.

"He told me that he didn't want to call us 'ma'am' and 'miss' anymore and that he wanted first names," said Nichole, noting that Edsel tracked employees' shifts at the facility with uncanny accuracy. "Someone would come in and he'd say, "Did you have a nice two days off?

"He knew."

Rose Mary Titler, R.N., was Edsel's Hospice nurse. "I just love him," she said. "He's a doll. He's taught me patience, understanding and compassion. We had to build trust, and that trust came very hard, something not easily conquered.

"We've developed quite a friendship and quite a relationship. He's one of a kind and I'll miss him. It'll be hard."

The day before Edsel died, he weighed barely 90 pounds. His color was bad and he was gaunt. When I touched him on the shoulder, all I felt was bone. He decided to go to the cemetery anyway.

Whatever issues Edsel may have had with his parents didn't prevent him from paying his respects one final time, and accompanied by his younger brother Robert, he made the trip in a minivan driven by Alesha.

She pulled up to Section J at Hillcrest Memorial Park, and Edsel waited in the passenger seat while Alesha and his brother and Debbie the social worker used brushes in an attempt to find the marker, flush with the ground and shrouded beneath snow and ice.

They were unsuccessful, but that didn't stop Edsel from saying a little prayer as he gazed out onto the tree-lined landscape. "You can say a little prayer anywhere," he said.

On the way home, he asked if he could have a Whopper, and it was no problem. The van made one more stop so Debbie could stock up on Edsel's favorite drink, Pepsi.

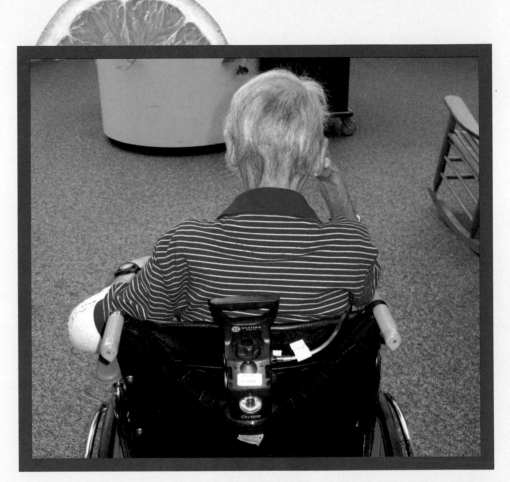

Edsel McDonald
1940 – 2011

She returned to the vehicle with two 8-packs of Coke instead. "I hope Coke's OK," she said.

Edsel turned and managed a little grin, grateful for small luxuries. "That's fine."

Elaine Martin holds a photo of her son Paul. "Moms always like to share pictures," she says.

AN ANGEL IN OUR MIDST—CELEBRATING THE JOYFUL LIFE OF PAUL MARTIN

She still sees his smiling face, hears his peals of laughter, even feels his touch.

Paul Martin left this world too soon, just one week shy of his 32nd birthday. But thanks to an uncommon bond between Paul and his mother, Elaine still has a sense that Paul is with her. She smiles softly. "All the time."

Paul—a Hope Network consumer during the latter part of his life—died in September 2010. But the love and joy he spread in his short time with us is cause to celebrate both the big and little moments that comprise our lives. Above all, he was happiest among others.

His glee was tied to two things. One, it was endemic to his syndrome. And two, he was the recipient of incredible patience and sacrifice showered down by parents who included Paul not only as part of their family, but the community at large.

Elaine and husband Mike noticed something out of the ordinary when Paul was just six months old. But it would be nearly 20 years before they came to understand the diagnosis that defined both the strange and wonderful characteristics exhibited by their firstborn.

Though often mistaken for combinations of autism and cerebral palsy, Paul had something instead called "Angelman Syndrome," a neuro-genetic disorder that occurs in just one of every 15,000 live births.

Paul reveling in Halloween fun

He was the last to walk down the aisle at his high school graduation. The applause was thunderous.

Paul often talked about Angels

Early on, Paul was prone to minor seizures, as many as two dozen or more in a single day. He never developed a sophisticated vocabulary, and his cognitive development didn't progress beyond that of a preschooler.

He presented other special challenges as a tot. "He didn't nap or sleep through the night for four years," Elaine remembers. "We were always, always exhausted. He was a joy to be around, except for 2 and 3 and 4 and 5 in the morning."

Elaine was working in a regional center for the developmentally disabled in Mt. Pleasant. More than once, "I found myself sitting on the floor of the bathroom, fast asleep."

She says "It usually took a couple of hours to get him to sleep, and then he'd only sleep for a couple of hours." Of staying up with him, she

117

recalls of herself and Mike that "We just took turns."

It became necessary to enlist the help of friends. "Please come over," a desperate Elaine would implore of a neighbor. "I'm afraid I'm gonna hurt him."

Dealing honestly with their needs and emotions endeared Elaine and Mike to a large contingent of people willing to help out, and that included students attending Central Michigan University, who spent time with Paul in an exchange for free room and board at the Martin house.

The family's cadre of friends only grew, in part because it was Paul's nature to engage virtually anyone with his smile and sense of play. He loved being outside, even in the dead of winter—delighting in plastic toys, gesturing where speech failed him, giving and scoring hugs.

A happy family: Paul with mom, dad and sister Kaye

He never sat in one place long. "Wanted to be hugged, but couldn't stand to be held," says Elaine. Paper fascinated him, and if someone was coming to visit, the couple would tell them "Bring a catalog," and Paul would tear into it page by page.

He also was smitten by water, and Mike and Elaine seized on the opportunity to teach him during bathtub time, "the only place he'd stay still." She'd hide things in the bubbles, and it's where he learned to sign key words and phrases.

Paul first attended classes at Lincoln School, then enrolled at Ottawa Middle before spending five years at Byron Center High

School, where he earned a certificate of completion on graduation day.

He was the last to walk the aisle, and the applause was thunderous. Nearly 100 attended his Open House, a preschool teacher included.

He made scads of friends during his teen years and longed especially to be around girls with blonde hair, mostly friends of his younger sister, Kaye, now 27 and studying in her mother's footsteps to become a speech pathologist.

Because Kaye graduated from Kelloggsville High, Paul was known and loved by two communities, a fixture at sports events, concerts and more. Says Elaine, "Everyone knew Paul."

People who met him rarely forgot him. As an adult, Paul encountered a gal at a summer camp for people with special needs. They'd been "peer pals" more than a decade earlier while she attended Riverside Elementary in Grand Rapids.

Now, she was working at the camp, and when Paul came through, she recognized him immediately, and reminded Paul and his parents of a journal she'd completed as part of the peer pal program. After all these years, she still had it. She gave it to Paul. Then, she shared that she was majoring in Special Education. Paul was the why.

No one saw his death coming. People with Angelman Syndrome can be expected to enjoy a typical life span. But last September, Paul was living at Hope Network's Mercy Respite Center and he had just boarded a van for an outing when he grew quiet, then fell sick.

He started vomiting and couldn't stop. He collapsed twice and was rushed to St. Mary's Mercy Medical Center, where his condition worsened.

He was admitted to intensive care, and a specialist who examined him told his shocked parents "There's nobody in this hospital sicker than your son," words that haunt Elaine to this day.

Tests confirmed Paul had septicemia, a grave infection of the blood. Doctors had hoped as a last resort to perform a colostomy, but before the procedure could get under way, Paul's heart stopped.

More than 300 paid their respect at the memorial service, held at Fredrik Meijer Gardens and Sculpture Park.

Recently, Paul's family sponsored a "Pig Out for Paul Party" that celebrated his incredible life and generous nature. More than 80 attended, and almost $600 was collected to present to Hope's Respite Center in Paul's name.

A year after his death, Elaine still misses the nights together when he'd settle down and they'd watch TV together, gently embraced.

Elaine works as a speech pathologist for Hope Network now, a job she relishes because she knows firsthand how Hope helps. At the 36th Street campus, where she keeps a tidy office, her only boy's smiling face glows from her computer's screensaver. Elaine's eyes well with tears. "This is my son, looking at me."

Sometimes, when she's alone in the car, she smiles to remember how he loved to just ride, and how he'd place her hand on the radio knob to search the kind of music that compelled him to rock back and forth as they drove.

"Every once in a while," says Elaine, "I find myself cranking up the music.

"And I just rock."

■ ■ ■ ■ ■ ■

Elaine gave this picture a title: "Just the two of us."
Paul always enjoyed a day at the beach, and Elaine loved to take him there.

The Prayer of Saint Francis

"O Lord, make me an instrument of Thy Peace!
Where there is hatred, let me sow love.
Where there is injury, pardon.
Where there is discord, harmony.
Where there is doubt, faith.
Where there is despair, hope.
Where there is darkness, light.
Where there is sorrow, joy.

Oh Divine Master, grant that I may not
so much seek to be consoled as to console;
to be understood as to understand;
to be loved as to love;
for it is in giving that we receive;
it is in pardoning that we are pardoned;
and it is in dying that we are born to Eternal Life."

To order additional copies of *The Book of CAKE,* or to explore bulk pricing, please contact cake@hopenetwork.org.

To request interviews with or appearances by the author, Tom Rademacher, contact cake@hopenetwork.org.

You are also invited to consult www.hopenetwork.org for additional information about our organization and how you can support our work.